PEOPLE
SOLVE
PROBLEMS

The Power of Every Person,
Every Day, Every Problem

JAMIE FLINCHBAUGH

People Solve Problems: The Power of Every Person, Every Day, Every Problem
Copyright © 2021 Jamie Flinchbaugh

Published by Old Dutch Group

Hardcover ISBN: 978-1-7376761-0-2
Paperback ISBN: 978-1-7376761-1-9
eISBN: 978-1-7376761-2-6

Cover and Interior Design: GKS Creative

Structural and Line Editing: Rob Worth

Copyediting and Proofreading: Kim Bookless

Illustrations: Laia Dausà

Project Management: The Cadence Group

This book is dedicated to every purpose-driven leader who aspires to craft an effective and resilient organization.

Contents

CONTENTS

CONTENTS

Foreword

AS PRESIDENT AND CEO of a leading technology company that's known for solving our customers' most difficult technical challenges, I've witnessed firsthand how people solve problems. When we began our lean journey shortly after the merger to form Qorvo in 2015, we called on Jamie Flinchbaugh to advise us. Jamie was already a recognized author and thought leader in lean, and as an executive consultant and coach, he helped us understand how lean and continuous improvement can be applied across a global organization—not just within manufacturing operations. Our goal was to get better to get bigger.

Working with Jamie, we established our cultural goals and began measuring the steady progress in our lean journey. One of the key early lessons he taught us is that acknowledging problems is the first step to solving them. We learned that it was OK to raise awareness of problems. Hiding problems only denies teams and individuals the opportunity to solve them. We soon discovered that Jamie's approach to problem solving isn't just theoretical but practical and can be applied across a growing tech company so that we could better serve our customers—the world's most demanding smartphone, networking, IoT, and defense system providers.

Once we witnessed the benefits of problem solving and lean in operational improvements and our financial results, we asked Jamie to join Qorvo's executive staff reporting to me as Corporate Vice President of our Lean Journey. We weren't asking him to solve our problems but to be an agent for change and to teach us how to lead in a lean operating environment. Our executive team recognized the axiom "For things to change, I must change."

As a member of Qorvo's staff, Jamie helped create a lean culture throughout Qorvo, driving continuous improvement initiatives in our two business units and within our general and administrative, selling and marketing, and other areas. He helped Qorvo establish and then build a community of lean leaders that continues to grow and now includes at least one leader for every function in the company. We now have a deep roster of problem solvers who are leading by example and enabling our global teams to share what we've learned across Qorvo, breaking down geographic and functional barriers.

One of my favorite quotes we learned from Jamie is this:

> Your beliefs will drive your behaviors,
>
> your behaviors will drive your actions,
>
> and your actions will generate results.

Beliefs and behavior *without* action won't deliver results. As a public company with over $4 billion in annual sales, we're graded every quarter based on our results. Those results are dependent and informed by the right beliefs and actions.

Our focus on lean is now producing measurable results. It has helped Qorvo eliminate waste, create more standard processes, and improve our quality, customer satisfaction, and financial performance. We've achieved this because we started at the top of the organization, focusing our energy on our leaders to help create a problem-solving culture. Not only have we reduced the time needed to design new products, we have now improved the time required to "close the books" every quarter without impacting accuracy.

In *People Solve Problems*, Jamie cuts through the labels and jargon of lean to focus on what can benefit every organization: getting better by allowing people to solve problems. He provides a practical framework that begins with behaviors, explores the steps needed to develop problem-solving capabilities and effective approaches to coaching, and underscores the critical role of active and engaged leaders.

People Solve Problems is a great roadmap for problem-solving success. As Jamie illustrates, it begins with defining the problem and the importance of establishing standards. Without standards, there is no way to measure improvement. Are you developing people-centered capabilities and testing solutions to learn as you go? Are you fostering a problem-solving culture where it's OK to expose and document problems? Finally, and most important, are leaders actively involved in problem solving? Have they played an active role in designing systems of work to expose, capture, manage, resource, and resolve problems?

Like his approach to business, Jamie's structured approach to problem solving in *People Solve Problems* is insightful and practical. While there are a lot of great business books available, including *The Hitchhikers Guide to Lean*, few are as actionable as this one.

In the words of legendary architect I. M. Pei, "Success is a collection of problems solved." Good luck on your own journey to problem-solving success.

BOB BRUGGEWORTH
President & CEO
Qorvo (Nasdaq: QRVO)

Introduction

Why did I write this book? When Andy Carlino and I wrote *The Hitchhiker's Guide to Lean*, we wanted to share ideas that no one else was writing about. We believed, as we still do today, that for lean to be successful, (1) it must be based on principles and behaviors, and (2) it must have not just support but leadership engagement. These challenges are not any easier to solve today, but they are at least now recognized as vital to true change in an organization. When we first started working together over twenty years ago, and when we wrote *The Hitchhiker's Guide to Lean*, these beliefs were not widely held. Lean was primarily focused on value stream mapping and *kaizen* events. We have come a long way, although I still talk about those primary two challenges, and we are pleased to see people still using and referring to our previous work.

We could let that book stand. Observant readers will notice the connections as we covered five Lean Principles. Systematic Problem Solving was one, right in line with this book. Direct Observation is a core capability necessary for good problem solving. One could argue that Systematic Waste Elimination is just another type of

1

problem solving. Of course, problem solving is nothing without High Agreement of Both What and How (often experienced as standardization), as either the starting point or ending point. And finally, problem solving is all about learning, and so the central principle of Create a Learning Organization is easily connected. Just like that, we have recapped chapter 1 of *The Hitchhiker's Guide to Lean.*

Why Not Stop There?

There are three reasons we're not stopping there. First, very few organizations start with principles. They start on the more practical side and often with something applicable and results-oriented, such as problem solving. They might be deploying agile methodologies, for example, but this only surfaces more problems that require the ability to work through them. This means problem solving is a stronger foundation on which a company can build a principle-based and leader-led transformation.

Second, not every organization is, wants to be, or should be investing in an explicit lean journey. Every organization, however, does problem solving at some level. There is nothing magical about declaring you are doing lean, and quite frankly, I do not think it should matter. There has been too much invested and wasted in labels, umbrella frameworks, and hierarchies of ideas. Most people and most companies just want to get better and be more in control of their own destiny. Every organization has people who solve problems. I hope this book makes many of these core ideas more accessible to those organizations.

Third, I wanted to explore problem solving more deeply than we had a chance to in our previous book. I have been doing exactly that through my coaching and my writing for many years, so if this isn't the pinnacle of that personal learning journey, this book is at least a comfortable plateau.

Much like *The Hitchhiker's Guide to Lean*, in writing *People Solve Problems: The Power of Every Person, Every Day, Every Problem*, I didn't want to write about topics that are already well covered. Problem solving as a tool and methodology is well covered. There are numerous books about it. Some of my favorites are *Understanding A3 Thinking: A Critical Component of Toyota's PDCA Management System* by Durward Sobek and Art Smalley, *Managing to Learn: Using the A3 Management Process to Solve Problems, Gain Agreement, Mentor, and Lead* by John Shook, *The Toyota Way Fieldbook* by Jeffrey Liker and David Meier, and, although a little different, *The High-Velocity Edge* by Steven Spear. If you want to learn more about the methods and tools of problem solving, these will serve as a good start. This book shouldn't be the only book you read on problem solving, but it will serve you well if it's one of your first two books on the topic.

I wanted to write about the gaps organizations experience that wrap around problem solving. If the problem-solving tool is the compass, then consider *People Solve Problems* the map. I cover topics not written about in the other books or taught in problem-solving classes. Most problem-solving courses begin right after you have pulled out the problem-solving tool and you're ready to start using it. This is similar to teaching someone how to live a healthy lifestyle by teaching them how to hold a dumbbell, when it's getting to the gym in the first place that is the gap worth bridging. This is the approach to this book. I want to write about getting you to the gym.

People Solve Problems: The Power of Every Person, Every Day, Every Problem is built on four primary domains. After setting up the challenge, we start by exploring People-Centered Capabilities.

These capabilities are tool agnostic, equally applicable to any chosen problem-solving method or no method at all. Next, we cover Problem-Solving Culture. These chapters outline the culture needed in the organization or the personal behaviors you must master to be successful in problem solving. Third, we dive into Success through Coaching. Problem solving is unlike other practices, training is incredibly insufficient, and coaching is the major driver of success. Finally, we explore the Role of the Leader, whether the CEO or a team leader, in building an environment where problem solving can thrive.

It is recommended that you read this book from beginning to end, as each chapter contains its own applicable nuggets of learning but the overall ecosystem is dependent on the other sections. However, the breakdown of these four sections also allows you to either read or teach your organization these ideas in clearly categorized lessons.

Who Did I Write This For?

For starters, I wrote this for myself. In fact, I do most of my writing for myself. This is selfish, and that is okay because if we don't care about our own personal learning, then no one else will do it for us. Writing has always been a way for me to converge and clarify my thinking into clear and salient ideas that I can use, teach, and coach.

Next, I wrote this for anyone wanting to improve themselves, their team, or their organization through problem solving. There are many use cases that I imagined while assembling content for this book, including leaders from the C-Suite on down, change agents, and individuals working on self-improvement.

For leaders at any level, this book provides a blueprint. The last section of the book, The Role of the Leader, is targeted toward you, and while you might not read the book backward, it is vital that you read this section to understand your role. Your role is much more than just solving bigger problems than your team solves. The book will also lay out expectations for the capabilities you need in your organization and the kind of culture you need to build.

For change agents, whether in a formal role such as a lean or agile team or informally working with a coalition, this book provides a roadmap to guide the transformation you desire. The section on coaching might be the centerpiece of your action plan, but the earlier sections provide a guide on what you are building, and the last section gives a clear description of what you are asking of the leaders in the organization.

For individuals who just want to improve, *People Solve Problems* provides a guide to both reflection and action that allows you to expand your horizons of problem solving beyond tools and methods. Start to look at your own work, your own capabilities, and your own behaviors. Then both invite in coaching and reach out through coaching, as I certainly believe that we learn even more about problem solving through coaching. And finally, use the section about leaders to help craft the right environment around you for success and work your way toward being able to deploy what you learned when you find yourself in a leadership role.

Enjoy the reading, learn and apply the lessons, and problem-solve your way to success.

SECTION 1

What Is the Problem
with Problem Solving?

1

Problem Solving
Is Not Just Tools

For anyone reading this who is familiar with my teaching, this first chapter will come as no surprise. Problem-solving tools are not the key to success. Behaviors are more important, more effective, and more powerful than the set of tools you use to execute problem solving. Twelve years ago, that was the premise of the first chapter of my book with Andy Carlino, *The Hitchhiker's Guide to Lean*. Twenty years ago, that was the premise of starting a company with Andy. The first chapter of our book was on lean principles. We argued that lean was not born from tools but from how we think.

This premise has been tested and broadly accepted throughout the lean community. That does not mean that everyone knows what to do with the idea but that many people believe principles and behaviors, otherwise known as culture, are a massive leverage point for the success of lean.

I was fortunate in my early experiences to reach this conclusion, although I did not articulate it clearly at the time. In the book *Practicing Lean*, I outlined my first deep experience with lean while at Harley-Davidson. Read my chapter in that book for the full story, but the short version is that while installing and running one of the first large-scale pull systems in North America, the majority of failure modes had nothing to do with the system design or the included tool kit; instead, failures were all about how people behaved using the system.

When it comes to problem solving, I believe the underlying concept that principles and behaviors matter more than the tool is even more powerful. Why? Because while many lean tools drive the work, problem solving is an even bigger challenge. It is a human challenge. People solve problems. There is no way around that. Tools do not solve problems. Methods do not solve problems. Data does not solve problems. We rely on the strengths and the weaknesses of people to solve problems.

Behaviors Drive Actions

There is a formula behind this key idea. Our principles and beliefs (how we think) drive our behaviors. Our behaviors, which can be described as a consistent pattern of actions across multiple situations, drive our actions in any particular situation. And our actions ultimately drive our results.

Let us walk backward through this to make sure we get it right. If a leader is focused only on results as the leverage in the organization, they will insist that their team "get better results." Sure, they might say it in an artful or inspiring way, but it is still only asking for better results. When a leader focuses on actions, especially in problem solving, they might ask people to "do more A3s" (a popular problem-solving method). How many times in a meeting do you hear a leader say, "Could we get an A3 on that?" or "I think that needs an A3." This is focused only on the action, in the moment, of doing more problem solving.

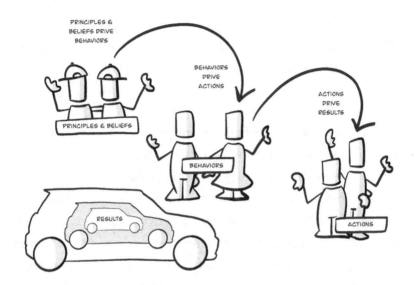

Digging below that has a greater impact. When focused on behaviors, a leader might be both a role model and coach for people to be curious about cause and effect. This will perhaps require that we use problem-solving methods to gain that understanding, but the focus is on the behavior of curiosity. And deeper still, a principle beneath that behavior is that problem solving is all about learning.

The leverage for sustainable and impactful gains is in the principles and behaviors. More often, I really focus on the behaviors rather than the principles. There are two primary reasons for this.

First, behaviors can be role-modeled. If I want to role-model problem solving for my team, they cannot see how I think or what I believe. However, they can observe my behaviors, especially if I'm conscientious about being a role model.

Second, behaviors are observable in the other direction. I can observe whether my team is adopting and practicing the desired behaviors. To drive change, a leader must be able to observe and evaluate whether they are getting the results they desire. It is quite difficult to observe someone's beliefs, but their behaviors are much more observable and a useful proxy for the thinking behind them.

How We Fail by Focusing on the Tools

There are many observable failure modes when the focus is too much on the tools of problem solving, and I will explore them in the chronological order in which they appear in your evolution. The first failure typically observed is what we call "malicious compliance." Malicious compliance is following rules or instructions but not as intended and sometimes with deliberately poor consequences. This is done either as a form of protest against the new requirement or simply not wanting to be bothered and therefore deliberately doing the bare minimum.

In problem solving, this usually looks like using the tool or method to document a preexisting conclusion. In these situations, the tool is used as a weapon of manipulation against any sense of its true intent or spirit. A long time ago, I had a maintenance manager who worked for me in our factory. In our operation, if you had at least one minute of downtime, you were required to complete a 5 Why Downtime Report. The form captured the instance and impact of the problem and required a 5 Why analysis to get to the root cause, and then a countermeasure needed to be documented and implemented. I had to review and approve any of the maintenance manager's reports. This maintenance manager was a tremendously talented electrician and truly cared about the operation as much as anyone. But he was also difficult, and anything that didn't resemble people staying out of his work was met with resistance and sometimes outright refusal. He lost the battle on complying with the 5 Why Downtime Report, so he tried malicious compliance. Every single report, whether it started with a broken-down conveyor or a failed robot, went through the 5 Why analysis and got to the same root cause: not enough resources. This allowed him to declare innocence, kick the problem up the organizational ladder, and still officially comply with the mandatory report.

This story might seem extreme, but I can promise every organization has some malicious compliance going on. Since getting the culture right is a "one heart and one mind at a time" journey, there will always be someone practicing malicious compliance that you haven't yet converted. But how many people? And for how long? By focusing on the behaviors of good problem solving, we can reduce this failure mode. People do not get "credit" for completing a problem-solving template; they get credit for practicing the right behaviors. This is obviously much harder, which we will get into later in the book, but it solves this and other failure modes.

The next failure mode that shows up is unthinking problem solving. Problem solving is a thinking person's game. People will "give it a shot" when the problem-solving template is thrust in front of them, but they are so focused on the tool that they don't think—they just complete it. A great way to determine whether this is how people are operating is by observing what happens when they get to a current reality or cause analysis part of the template. At this point, someone will capture what they already know. They will start writing down bullet points of all the things they know about the problem. But what they already know is not likely to be where the insight or solution comes from. This behavior comes from a compelling drive to get through the template and complete the task.

In one extreme case years ago, we did some analysis and determined that a team I was working with would have a lot of resistance and frustration with any tool or template. Instead of a tool, we just focused on problems and the skills and next steps of trying to tackle them. We worked on the right behaviors and built the right skills. After about six months and several iterations, the team came to me and said, "We've noticed a pattern in a lot of the problem solving we've done, so we put together this template to capture them in the future." It looked a lot like an A3 template (imagine that!), just a little less tightly packaged. This team never focused on the template but instead on what they needed to do to overcome problems. This is not an approach I would take with most organizations, but it demonstrates how a team can truly learn without needing a tool.

The third failure mode is related to the last one but usually occurs after they have overcome it. This failure mode is treating problem solving linearly as a series of steps. Many times, problem solving is even taught in numbered steps, such as 8-Step Problem Solving, which can exacerbate this behavior. A person will begin problem solving, starting with step one, and diligently complete each step in turn. The trouble is that effective problem solving is rarely linear. You learn something in one step that takes you back a step for modification. Or you test an idea, and it doesn't produce the intended result, so you test the next solution on your list or perhaps restudy the cause of the problem. A great test of this is the problem statement itself. Ask someone how often their problem statement was modified after starting. If they never say yes, then it is likely they are treating it as a linear process instead of embracing the problem with the right behaviors and deploying the right skills.

The final failure mode is one we observe further into the journey when many people are more mature in using their methodology. I have said for a long time that if we could measure it, the best gauge of a successful journey is that there are more informal and voluntary efforts than formal and forced efforts. You want the informal to be greater in number than the formal (although not just by reducing the formal, of course). When this happens with problem solving, you see templates written on whiteboards, 5 Whys on the backs of envelopes, and deep dives being done at the point of activity through a discussion between two individuals. When we focus on the tools, this never happens, either because people want credit for their activity or simply because they can't see past the tool because the tool is the template. This will permanently limit your ability to build a truly high-momentum problem-solving organization.

Regardless of which tools and templates you have selected, the critical behaviors and capabilities of problem solving are universal. In section 2, I will break down the skills in People-Centered Capabilities. In section 3, I explore both the individual and organizational behaviors in Problem-Solving Culture. In section 4, I go deeper into the most effective approach to building those capabilities and behaviors in Success through Coaching. Finally, section 5 describes The Role of the Leader in the context of problem solving. You will notice there is no section on problem-solving tools. Does this mean tools are unimportant?

2

Don't the Tools Matter?

Tools do matter. Just not as much as we are led to believe.

In the 1980s, MacGyver was a popular television show that featured the problem-solving skills of its title character. MacGyver would get out of ridiculous situations using his inventiveness, his knowledge of science, and whatever was lying around. As a future engineer, this kind of show really appealed to me. Besides the fact that the science and engineering weren't always valid, he rarely had the proper tools to solve the problem apart from his trusty pocket-knife, which always removed one variable from the situation. While entertaining, MacGyver didn't really use the best solutions for the problems at hand. Perhaps this is what led to *Saturday Night Live* doing a parody called MacGruber, where he repeatedly fails and blows up. MacGyver seemed to be proof that you didn't need the right tools, but they certainly help.

While this might seem like a silly analogy, if you gave me Yo-Yo Ma's multimillion-dollar cello or Wynton Marsalis's trumpet and then gave them a kazoo, who is more likely to create better music? Of course, it would be them, because their talent and thinking come from within.

However, give them a better tool to demonstrate those talents, and their performance gets better still. Tools do matter.

Still, my experience having worked with over three hundred companies throughout my coaching and consulting career suggests that the tools are not the differentiator. There are two primary observations. First, if I consider the organizations I have worked with and compare the best problem-solving organizations with some of the very worst, they often use the same tools. If the problem-solving tools made a major difference, then you would expect some correlation between the selected tool set and success, but I have found none. Second, the five or ten best problem-solving organizations all used either slightly or significantly different tools. To be fair, some of them did use the same starting point, but they evolved their tool set over time, either to incorporate what they had learned or to help overcome gaps in their practice.

This leads me to what is probably one of my more controversial opinions when it comes to problem solving. Organizations that either build or modify their own problem-solving methods over time are inherently stronger.

There are two reasons for this. First, at a meta level, they are practicing problem solving on their problem-solving efforts, and sometimes part of their improvements involves changing the methodology or templates used. Toyota is a company that is in the top tier of problem solving and is often copied, but people can miss this adaptive aspect of their history.

Second, by constructing your own problem-solving method, its architects (who will probably end up as your best coaches) understand the reasons behind the construction. Their understanding of why the method works is powerful knowledge. This is why, for example, during much of my two engineering master's degrees, I was required to rediscover important formulas that had already been derived. I could just use the formula, but by having to reconstruct the thought process, I certainly better understand why and how the formula worked.

A Brief Tour of the Tools

People Solve Problems is written as a tool-agnostic book. I might have my favorite tools, but I have written this with the intent of helping organizations regardless of their tool set. Perhaps every method has some strengths and weaknesses, and some of the best problem solvers I know have at least studied, and often continue to use, a range of different tools.

Consider the method we all start with: "trying stuff." This might not be a method we would teach, but we all have done it and usually still utilize it throughout our life. It is best to call it what it is. We aren't taught how to crawl, but we want to get somewhere (the problem statement) and keep wiggling around until we move. We then discover "Hey, that works," and continue to do more of it, and before you know it, we are crawling. Then we move on to the next problem:

how to unlock Mom's cellphone! Trying stuff doesn't usually involve well-crafted problem statements or any study of why things work. We are simply looking for empirical evidence that an action produces the results we want. We should acknowledge that this is part of our problem-solving arsenal.

My personal journey took me to engineering school, first as an undergraduate at Lehigh University and later master's degrees at the University of Michigan and MIT. I learned a lot about problem solving throughout my engineering education. There were numerous tools in the tool set (such as the six statistics courses I took throughout my education) and, of course, many skills learned as well. Most engineers would claim proficiency in problem solving, although generally that is limited to technical problems.

When I arrived at Chrysler, I was quickly taught the Kepner-Tregoe set of tools and templates, along with a handy file folder where I carried preprinted templates. This was a branded and trademarked problem-solving tool set created by the eponymous company, which still says on the front of its website:[1] "Become a Leader in Problem Solving." Their Problem Analysis method, for example, includes the following steps:

- Problem Overview
- Further Description
- State the Problem
- Specify the Problem
- Use Distinctions and Changes
- Identify Possible Causes

---

1   "Become a Leader in Problem Solving," Kepner-Tregoe, accessed June 30, 2021, http://kepner-tregoe.com.

- Test Possible Causes

- Determine Most Probable Cause

- Confirm True Cause

- Think Beyond the Fix

That is just Problem Analysis, but students of any problem-solving method will see some similarities, which returns to my point that the variations among the methods are less differentiated than many believe.

TQM, or Total Quality Management, included problem-solving training that spanned the globe. Although I took courses and read many books, much of what I learned came from Shoji Shiba and Dave Walden, two of the authors of *A New American TQM*.[2] While TQM was much broader than just problem solving, its teaching would often be accompanied by the 7 Basic Quality Tools,[3] which included cause-and-effect diagrams (also called a fishbone or Ishikawa diagram), check sheets, control charts, histograms, Pareto charts, scatter diagrams, and stratification.

Many more tools have been deployed, each with its own emphasis and strength. The DMAIC (Define, Measure, Analyze, Improve, Control) methodology, featured as the centerpiece of Six Sigma, emphasized careful analysis of data. TRIZ is a method that leverages in-depth studies of invention, including those that occur in nature, to help inspire creativity in solutions. 8D, or 8 Disciplines, was created by the Ford Motor Company and is often used specifically to help contain and solve product-quality escapes that get to a downstream

---

2   Shoji Shiba, Alan Graham, and David Walden, *New American TQM: Four Practical Revolutions in Management* (New York, Productivity Press, 1993).
3   "The 7 Basic Quality Tools for Process Improvement," American Society for Quality (ASQ), accessed June 30, 2021, https://asq.org/quality-resources/seven-basic-quality-tools.

supplier. Design Thinking, more popular in design and entrepreneur-
ial domains, gained a following through design consulting firm IDEO
and is particularly well-suited for vaguely defined problems, often
referred to as "wicked" problems.

A3 and 8-Step Problem Solving are two sides of the same coin,
often referring to exactly the same thing but sometimes divergent
in how they are adopted and adapted in different environments,
including within the origins of Toyota. A3 gets its name from the
standard-sized sheet of paper (close to 11"x17", the standard found
in the United States) used to capture the summary of effort. In fact,
at Toyota, it began as A3 Report Writing and was a standard only
for reporting on problem-solving efforts, not for actually solving the
problem. Because the format inherently had to capture the patterns
of thought and work behind their problem solving, it grew in meaning
into a problem-solving method. 8-Step refers to eight specific steps
in the problem-solving process, specifically:

- Clarify the problem

- Break down the problem

- Set the target

- Analyze the root cause

- Develop countermeasure

- Implement countermeasure

- Monitor results and process

- Standardize and share success

Just as with almost any process documenting problem solving
as steps, you can either break this down further or combine steps.
For example, are "standardize" and "share success" a single thing in

step eight? Of course not. Problem solving is complex and messy, and all these tools, frameworks, and lists help, but when taken too prescriptively, they can hurt as well.

Looking at A3s and 8-Step as the heart of Toyota's success is a mistake. As Tracey and Ernie Richardson describe their Toyota experience in their book *The Toyota Engagement Equation:*[4]

When it came to describing our approach, we didn't call it anything. It was just understood that this was our J-O-B. It wasn't until Toyota documented the Toyota Way in 2001 that words, labels, and so forth surfaced—and surged. This was a necessary step for maintaining Toyota's values, principles, and methods in a growing global organization, but it's important to remember that labels have limitations, particularly when it comes to creating something as intimate as Toyota's work culture. The danger here is falling into the "tools only" approach that's all too common in organizations that seek to emulate Toyota.

Toyota didn't start by creating and deploying the problem-solving tools that are now taught out of Toyota as the key to their success. They started by solving problems. They developed capabilities to do so over decades, with a mindset and behaviors that guided them. A3s and 8-Steps are all ways to try to codify and teach what they had already learned to do. How do you copy Toyota's success? I would argue it's not by copying where they are now but copying their journey, which means earning the knowledge for yourself through experience-based learning.

---

4   Tracey Richardson and Ernie Richardson, *The Toyota Engagement Equation: How to Understand and Implement Continuous Improvement Thinking in Any Organization* (New York: McGraw-Hill Education, 2017), introduction.

Why Use Tools?

After all of this, why should you use tools and methods for problem solving at all? There are benefits, but we should be clear and purposeful about those benefits so our actions fulfill their purpose.

THERE IS BENEFIT IN USING TOOLS, BUT WE SHOULD BE CLEAR AND PURPOSEFUL ABOUT THOSE BENEFITS, SO THAT OUR ACTIONS FULFILL THE PURPOSE

First, they act as job aids. Standards that *aid* the human being in the right behaviors and skills can help improve the consistency and efficacy of problem solving. The hierarchy matters. Humans are aided by the job aid versus serving the template. Tools and templates should enable human talent, not hinder it. When tools are treated as aids to the process, then the human being still owns the problem, how they engage with it, and ultimately what skills, insights, and creativity they bring to the problem. Problem solving is still a people-centric activity, but people can benefit from the right tools to help them perform at their best.

Second, they act as a standard through which to coach and teach. If I declared to everyone in the organization that they should start coaching, then the organization will move forward but in many different directions. The principles, behaviors, and skills should form the foundation of such standards, but the tools provide a canvas on which to collaborate. In the Success through Coaching section of the book, I explain how effective coaching gives the coachee, or student, the ability to learn through self-discovery. The tools provide some guardrails to help guide that self-discovery, while the coach focuses on both Guiding and Reflection in the learning process.

Third, the standard tools, and in particular their templates, help the reader of problem-solving efforts to know how to interpret what they are reading. Those reading or reviewing problem-solving results could have multiple purposes. They could be an internal or external customer of the process who cares about the outcome. They could be an executive or manager who is accountable for the outcome. They could be a collaborator who must be involved in implementing the solution. And finally, they could be a coach who is using the template to help assess what their coachee is doing well and what they could improve.

Tools have a place and a purpose, and just because they are more visible than the behaviors and capabilities of problem solving doesn't mean they deserve a higher position in the hierarchy of what matters.

3

The Marriage of Problem Solving and Standards

Standards and standardization have an entwined relationship with problem solving. For discussion purposes, standards, by my definition, cover everything from a documented and trained written procedure to the fact that your car's gas cap clicks, preventing both over- and under-tightening. Depending on your training lineage, that relationship may be unexplored or driven home as a mantra. Taiichi Ohno, the father of the Toyota Production System, is often quoted as saying, "Where there is no standard, there can be no *kaizen*," (*kaizen* is a commonly used Japanese word that means continuous improvement). This works great on a bumper sticker, or more commonly, on a PowerPoint slide, but there is much nuance to this statement that is not captured in the quote.

This is not a book on standards. There are plenty of books on that topic. However, since the link between standards and problem solving cannot be ripped apart, I wanted to spend just one chapter putting them in the context of one another.

Why Do Standards Matter?

Too much variation in the work you are trying to problem-solve presents multiple challenges. First, which of the near-infinite variations of the process created the problem condition you want to solve? Second, in analyzing the cause, do you ignore the variation or look at all of it? And perhaps most important, if you generate a great solution but can apply it only to a sea of variation, then what have you really changed? The stability of a standard provides a foundation for both the front end and the final stages of problem solving.

If you truly have no standard, then that is the gap you must close. Standards have benefits, but it is important to know what benefit or benefits you are trying to achieve so they can be developed properly. Otherwise, you might go ahead and standardize everything without end. Here are some clear benefits, and you can use them to shape what and how far you standardize.

First is simply performance gains. If one person or team can accomplish a task in one hour that takes everyone else three hours, then copying that best practice across multiple resources will provide tremendous gain. If there is a best-known method that produces a clearly superior result, then not standardizing is a conscious decision to accept losses. A key leadership question to those not adopting such a standard could be: "Why are you willing to accept substandard performance?"

Second is the ability to spot problems or abnormal conditions. This is a version of performance gains but is about maintaining the level of performance. This rationale applies when problems are likely to occur, and the best way to spot them is to see deviations from the standard. For example, during my standard drive to the airport, I know how long it should take me and where I face traffic or no traffic.

If there is a deviation from that standard, it is both easy to spot and important to identify at the earliest possible time. This reason could be applied to a wide range of situations, but be sure that (a) it is the best fit and (b) you achieve this level of outcome of being able to spot the abnormal condition.

Third is avoiding duplication of work. In other words, do not reinvent the wheel. If someone creates a tool or training materials, then every other team creating their own version is duplicating work that can be avoided. This is waste. If it takes one thousand hours to develop a new training package, even if another group might do it slightly better, it may not be worth duplicating one thousand hours' worth of work. If there is a cloud-based, off-the-shelf software application that can accomplish 80 percent of what you need to accomplish, is creating your own worth the additional 20 percent gain? Standards prevent waste.

Fourth is creating an environment that is conducive to flexible resources. If the demands on different teams vary, whether it is design teams, production teams, or call-center teams, it can be very useful to shift resources from team to team or site to site. If the methods of each team differ, the losses from someone shifting teams and learning new methods can offset the gains of the moved resource. If there are standard methods, then there are only gains rather than losses when shifting resources to optimize the total organizational output.

Fifth is supporting shared resources. If an important and shared resource has to work with several different groups, but with each group they have to change their approach, methods, communication, and so on, it is both inefficient and error-prone. Imagine if you had a company campus with employees moving between buildings, but each building established its own security system. What if the sales team, the design team, the planning team, and the production team all used different codes for their different products? The more differences from group to group, the harder it is for other groups to engage them all. This reason may be the most often abused, as we can force standardization on many for the efficiency of a select few without understanding or articulating the cost.

The final reason is being able to leverage shared learning. If two groups have a common method, then experiments and improvements can be leveraged across them. Controlled experiments can be run, abnormalities filtered out, and benefits leveraged. Without a common standard, every shared learning and experiment is justifiably discounted by saying, "That doesn't apply here." Note that this is the same as the first reason in spirit, but it is about future improvements versus improvements already accomplished.

Before you go through the effort of standardization, make sure you understand and articulate the benefit of your investment.

To What Level of Breadth and Depth Do We Build Standards?

In a certain way, this is where the Ohno quote we started the chapter with falls apart. If you are currently doing a task in a slightly consistent way, then you have a standard. Is the standard shared with others? If not, then it is not a broad standard. Is your way consistent in every single detail? If not, then it lacks depth of detail.

As a comparison, I have a standard for changing a tire. It is only slightly more detailed than the one provided in the owner's manual, with my own small improvements such as always carrying a heavy blanket (as versatile in a car trunk as a pocketknife is in your pocket) to lie or kneel on while performing the task. The standard is not broadly adopted, as only in teaching one of my kids would it really get deployed any further than myself. It also lacks depth because there are many details that get figured out in the moment. Now compare that to a NASCAR or Formula One pit crew changing a tire. It has breadth, not only across all members of the team, but certain aspects are standard across all teams through a combination of the rulebook and competitive benchmarking. It is also very detailed, down to how to position your toes so that you can move from position to position more quickly. The difference in the levels of breadth and depth of the standard is driven by the benefits stated earlier in the chapter.

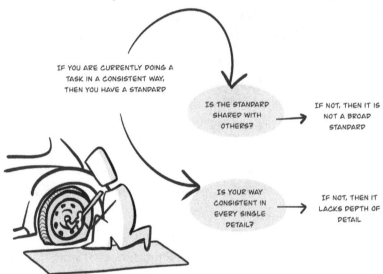

IF YOU ARE CURRENTLY DOING A TASK IN A CONSISTENT WAY, THEN YOU HAVE A STANDARD

IS THE STANDARD SHARED WITH OTHERS? → IF NOT, THEN IT IS NOT A BROAD STANDARD

IS YOUR WAY CONSISTENT IN EVERY SINGLE DETAIL? → IF NOT, THEN IT LACKS DEPTH OF DETAIL

The premise of Ohno's quote is valid but hardly ever completely true. It is really a matter of degrees, in both breadth and depth. Of those challenging the lack of depth or detail, many will point to the lack of a documented standard. However, is a documented standard inherently better than one that isn't documented? That is really the wrong question, because it is not the document but the reality of the activity that determines the true standard.

I worked with a factory team that brought together technicians and engineers to look at the standards for preventive maintenance tasks. The technicians claimed there were no standards. The engineers insisted there were standards. The engineers would consistently point to a detailed document (that they usually wrote) that outlined everything you ever needed to know. The technicians would point out that the document was unusable, hadn't been opened, and certainly wasn't followed. Observations suggested that each technician and each shift had learned their own ways to do the job. The true observable reality of a situation has a funny way of cutting through the theoretical debate.

Another pushback comes from the other end, when people insist they have a standard and can point to a standard document. I will challenge them on whether their standard is the same as the one used in the next team, function, shift, or business unit. They do have a standard, but it is not adopted broadly enough to capture the benefits outlined earlier in this chapter.

Local context matters. A standard process that you follow at 2:00 p.m. may not work at 2:00 a.m. because the same resources are not in the building. A standard process that a pit crew of five people follows doesn't work when one person is injured and now it is four people. A standard process of how to engage a supplier doesn't work the same way for the $1 billion suppliers as it does for the $1 million suppliers. This limits our ability to achieve the depth and breadth that many lean advocates would desire. As lean thinker Michael Ballé wrote:

There are far fewer standards than situations. When in doubt, start with the standard where you have one, and apply your creativity to all other situations where the standard is unclear or inexistent. Standards are rare peaks of certainty on a few islands of "we think it's this way but we're not absolutely sure" in oceans of "we don't have a clue." So don't

start by challenging standards—there's plenty more fruitful to explore.[5]
Standards are not a binary outcome. You don't just either have a standard or don't have a standard. There is tremendous variation on how much depth or detail you have standardized and how broadly you have adopted the standard. Let us focus on that fact rather than the binary Shakespearian version: To standardize, or not to standardize, that is the question.

The Learning Pathway

Another factor to consider in the marriage of problem solving and standardization is how people learn about it. Of course, we can teach people all of this, through books and classes and on-the-job training, but that's only the input. The output is what they choose to internalize as beliefs. Logically, we want to teach people how to build standards before we teach them how to solve problems. This approach is often met with resistance. There are many reasons for this, including the fact that standardization is not a very exciting topic. People don't want to learn standardization. We can force them to learn how to standardize, but again, that doesn't mean they internalize the value of it.

I have found that many people learn to appreciate standards through the pathway of learning problem solving. This lesson is not always accomplished through self-study but through self-discovery under the guidance of a coach, which is why the later section, Success through Coaching, is so vital. There are two experiences, achieved over and over, that allow the student to learn the value of standards.

---

5   Michael Ballé, "Standards vs. Standardization," Lean Enterprise Institute, May 25, 2011, https://www.lean.org/balle/DisplayObject.cfm?o=1832.

First, in the early stages of problem solving, their ability to craft a problem statement (our next chapter) and their ability to diagnose the current state of the situation (the chapter after that) is more difficult if there is no standard. As stated in the benefits section above, standards make it easier to spot both abnormal conditions and their causes.

Second, once the problem solver wants to implement a solution, how do they implement the standard without standards? Whether hard coding the standard into software or a physical solution, or implementing it through a written and trained standard procedure, a solution without a standard is merely a suggestion. After solving problem after problem, the problem solver learns to appreciate standardization.

Standards and problem solving are intertwined, and although that is a subject I could explore much more deeply, for the purposes of *People Solve Problems*, I wanted to make the context of the relationship clear before we proceed any further.

SECTION 2

People-Centered Capabilities

In this section, we explore the highest leverage capabilities that an individual or an organization can develop. You will notice these capabilities are tool agnostic. No matter which tool you are using, or no tool at all, these capabilities still apply. When you think about the daily conversations that occur "off the page" in meetings, hallways, or one-on-ones that never involve pulling out a template, each one of the capabilities applies. In general, they are presented in a sequence consistent with how they might appear in a problem-solving method, but keep in mind that problem solving is not granular and so each of the capabilities can be called on at any moment.

4

Creating Problem Statements

If there were a single skill that I could extract from problem solving and get into the hands of people all over the world, it would be the ability to craft a good problem statement. This is one of—if not *the*—most valuable skills. Making matters worse, it is one of the least taught and often is treated as a small step in formal problem solving, necessary only because you have to fill out a template. Yet almost every methodology previously mentioned includes some aspect of defining the problem that needs to be solved.

The same repeated observation tells me about both its value and the current capability gap. Put five to ten people into a room to engage on a problem. Ask everyone, "What is the problem?" You will get as many answers as you have people. This speaks to its value because how can you possibly have a team of people collaborate effectively on solving a problem if they cannot even agree on what the problem is?

Crafting effective problem statements not only improves problem solving but it helps the many close cousins of problem solving, such as creating goals and objectives, designing metrics, leading innovation, selling something, developing a strategy, and designing products. Each of these is a form of problem solving, and each depends on well-framed problem statements.

What Is a Problem Statement?

No one should bring a proposal forward without determining what problem they are trying to solve. This should become a habit for your organization, and it should become an expectation from leaders.

The easiest explanation of a problem statement is the existence of a gap between the current condition and the expected condition. The expected condition could be a clear standard of how a process should work or even a desired condition that you have not yet achieved. Regardless, you have a clearly defined gap, and problem solving is about closing that gap. The reason problem statements are so important as gaps is that you don't want to meander aimlessly through improvement, or make too small a change, or get stuck in the endless pursuit of an ill-defined goal.

Think of a problem statement as a vector. A vector has both direction and magnitude, and a problem statement defines both elements.

In which direction do we need to improve, and how far do we have to go to get there?

The direction of the vector, or problem statement, defines how we must move forward with other capabilities, such as understanding cause and effect, and even experimentation. Do we want to reduce defects or increase the speed of detecting them once created? Do we want to improve the average time to delivery or improve our worst time to delivery? Do we want to improve our hiring or our retention? The differences in these, when taken forward, can be incredibly significant. If you change the angle of a vector by just one degree, when you get to the end of it, you may be in a very different place. For example, if you own a pizza shop, improving the speed of pizza delivery sounds like a straightforward problem statement. However, solving the typical Friday night one-topping one-pizza delivery is a very different problem statement than improving the speed of a ten-pizza order on Super Bowl Sunday. Every step that follows will be affected by this difference.

The magnitude matters a great deal as well. If a doctor told you that you had to lose weight, the difference between ten and a hundred pounds has a profound impact on your approach. Do you need to improve lead times by 5 percent or 50 percent? Do you need to reduce costs by 5 percent or 25 percent? Once you understand the magnitude, then what you study, how you study, and what you are willing to consider for solutions can be dramatically different. Some might advocate to "just go for the bigger goal," but when the needs (usually of the customer) don't demand that, then there is always time to continue to progress—but framing the problem around the bigger gap can be tremendously wasteful to the organization. At a minimum, it takes resources away from another gap that must also be solved today.

Understanding the difference between a gap to standard performance and a gap to an expectation is an important distinction.
Fundamentally, working on a gap to a standard performance or a
standard result means you had a stable level of performance that is
no longer successful and you must return to that condition. This is
often driven by a metric and can be defined by a clear, measurable
magnitude. A gap in expectation is more often about raising the bar
to a new need or expectation. This requires a new level of performance, previously unachieved. But it still comes from a need, not an
arbitrary raising of the bar just to see whether people can leap over it.

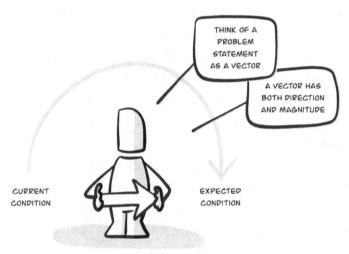

Getting Started

Before you get into the problem statement itself, it is useful to frame
what kind of problem we're talking about and ensure we don't start
solving imagined problems. When a problem occurs, there are three
questions that must always be asked, and in this order. Chapter 3
helped set up the importance of these questions because they relate
to how standards and problem solving are connected.

1. Do we have a standard process?

If the answer is no, then stop there. You have found your gap. If there is no standard process or method, then you cannot problem-solve why the gap to standard exists. The only expectation you have failed is that you do not have a standard process, and that is now the gap you must close.

2. Did we follow the standard process?

If no, then pause before you jump in to try to improve the standard. If someone chose not to follow it, then that is your gap. There are many other legitimate reasons why someone may not have followed the standard process, and they all can result in a problem-solving gap. They may not have known the standard, or may not have understood it, and then you have a gap related to how the standards are deployed and trained. Perhaps the person or team did not have what they needed, such as tools, time, resources, or even information in order to follow the standard. In this case, you have found a gap that can be solved. The trickiest one to overcome is one of perception; they may have decided not to follow the standard because previously it has not worked. If you don't yet have a trusted problem-solving culture, then their work-around is simply to ignore the standard and do it some other way. However, this reason is very different from someone simply choosing not to follow it.

3. If we have a standard process and we used it, then what is wrong with the standard process?

Most problem-solving training focuses on this kind of problem, but we should not overlook the first two questions and start here. You are probably going to make things worse by solving the wrong factor.

These are important questions to ask before you jump to the wrong problem statement. These are the three types of problems.

Breaking Down the Problem

This is an element of the skill that shouldn't be so important but is crucial in framing the problem. If we engage everyone in our organization to find a problem and fix a problem, then problems are already broken down. Find the occurrence, or better still, observe the occurrence, and the problem is already broken down. You have seen the specific failure, and that makes it far more efficient to find the specific solution. You solve the problem that is in front of you.

Aggregating problems into bigger problem statements may be one of the biggest failures of today's management. We love big problems, and if we cannot find one, we will manufacture one (even if we're blind to it occurring). We have a budget problem, a sales problem, a product performance problem, or a personnel problem, but it is not that simple. In reality, there are a hundred budget problems or a thousand sales problems. This is not to diminish the importance of a large gap, but you cannot solve a hundred problems with one solution. It is vital that we understand each cause, each condition, and each occurrence if we are to solve the problems with any effectiveness.

One of the driving forces behind this is our sense of accomplishment, whether it is an internal drive or how the organization treats accomplishment. You wake up one Tuesday morning with a hundred potential problems to solve, so you find the biggest one possible so your effort is worth your time. You are more likely to be the hero if you solve a truly epic problem. However, we then deceive ourselves in framing the big problem, even though it is not one problem at all. We feel good that we are tackling it, but because it is like solving world hunger by searching for a single solution, our efforts are either disappointing or unending.

We are far better off with three (or fifty) distinct problem statements that all happen to have the same solution than one aggregated problem statement. If I happen to have a sore knee and a sore shoulder (as is often the case for me), then a single anti-inflammatory may solve both problems. However, if I have multiple ailments and fail to understand each unique one, then taking that same pill will lead to failure. It is not important that each unique problem has a unique solution, but it is important to understand each unique problem. This is why the problem statement is so important.

Sometimes we do not start off with a problem already broken down, so that leaves us two choices, both of which require some intuition. We can break down the problem using data. We can understand all the different occurrences and use data to find the greatest leverage. For example, if I am coaching my soccer team (I have coached soccer for thirty-five years, and this won't be the last analogy I use) and trying to solve the problem of not enough goals, I can analyze the times we failed to take a shot, the times we took the shot but missed the target, the times we failed to produce enough velocity on the shot, and the other times we failed with precise accuracy. Each one is a different problem statement, and finding the leverage provides me more focus to design effective solutions.

Sometimes we break down the problem systematically, meaning we understand the elements of the problem: what parts we are trying to solve and what parts we are not trying to solve. For example, if we are experiencing defect escapes from our process, we start to understand the contributing elements, such as the fragility of the design, the lack of control of the process, and the ability to detect the defect and prevent escapes. These are three different problem statements, and understanding each is critical to making progress. Solving the original problem may not be the most effective or efficient problem to solve. But what is most important to understand is that they are different problem statements.

We also want to seek out smaller problem statements. This helps us move faster, because smaller and more precise problems are faster and easier to solve. This is one of the benefits. The other is that when our problem statements are too big, we mix the problems and therefore the causes, making clean solutions less possible. Smaller, more focused problem statements are conclusively more effective.

Problem Statement Failure Modes

There are many observable failure modes when it comes to crafting problem statements. The most obvious is that we include the solution in the problem statement. "Needs to be automated" or "lack of proper equipment" are types of phrases we must watch out for. There are many times where the problem solver truly does adopt a problem statement—such as "We need this software,"—but that's not what they write in the template. The problem statement for them is just a thought, a thought about the need for a predetermined solution. That problem statement shapes the rest of the work, and even though they write something that sounds more like a problem statement in the template, all their work was indeed driven by the included-solution problem statement.

Avoiding too many causes, or causes with large leaps, in the problem statement is another failure mode. It is extremely hard to avoid this all the time because often, even with the most experienced practitioners, the observation of linkage is very clear on the first cause. For example, you might want to improve productivity, but the observations have made it obvious leading up to problem solving that interruptions are a massive cause. It does not have to be the whole issue, or even the biggest issue, but you pursue a problem statement of reducing interruptions by 90 percent. Technically, you made a leap from the outcome (productivity) to a cause (interruptions), but it is still an informed leap based on your observations (which we will cover in the next chapter). The risk is, when your jumps into the cause go too far, they are not informed by rigorous observation or study, and you make leaps that others are not aligned with.

Another failure mode in crafting problem statements is when they are not even defined as a gap. An example might be that "The process should be faster," or "The process is broken." In the first example, it is an easier fix because we can convert "faster" into a defined gap. The reason people write it that way is they do not know how fast it is going currently or how fast it should go—and often both—but they are at least certain it is not fast enough. This is reasonable, but it makes for a poor problem statement. In my coaching, I encourage people to write, "The process currently takes X and should take Y." This still means we don't know what the specific gap is, but it keeps us focused while learning through the other steps to figure out what X and Y need to be. The second version is more difficult. "Broken" cannot be quantified into what percent broken. Often this means we have lots of complaints and frustrations with a process, but we do not yet understand the frustration well enough to convert it into a problem statement. I often find this work must begin by gathering multiple problem statements through socialization, and that will help advance the understanding. Ultimately, those problem statements need to be refined, selected, and agreed on with everyone involved.

And this brings us to our final failure mode: there is no agreement about the gap. I remember once coaching a team that had completed their problem-solving effort, but they could not get the site director to agree with their solution. We went back through their entire process, including their analysis, and it was very well done. I finally asked, "Does the site director agree that this gap is actually a problem?" The answer was no. In this case, it did not matter how effective their problem solving was; it was a fruitless effort.

If those involved do not agree with the problem statement, then there is little hope of progress. For example, if someone doesn't see their smoking as a problem, then it isn't about finding the right strategy to quit. They must agree it is a problem before any strategy will even get adopted, let alone be effective. While observation and data can help you generate that alignment, there is still a bit of socialization needed to ensure there is alignment on the gap you are trying to solve. If you think being 5 percent behind schedule is a problem and I believe we are not behind schedule until we are 20 percent behind, we may agree on the fact that we are currently at 10 percent, but we will not agree it is a problem that should be solved. This alignment on what is a problem and what is not a problem is essential for success.

John Dewey, whose philosophy on problem solving is the basis of most modern problem solving going back 110 years, made this statement: "A problem well-defined is a problem half-solved." Yet we have seen for the last century that both individuals and teams slide right past the problem statement, investing extraordinarily little time on its definition.

I have found that appreciation for Dewey's statement comes much faster from people who coach problem solving rather than people who just execute a lot of problem solving. This is because coaches are above or beyond the problem itself. It is easier for them to see the common failure modes that multiple teams go through. Susan Pleasant, one of my favorite coaches and a former business partner of mine, used Dewey's statement in her email signature for years as a nod to exactly how important his point is.

This chapter is first in this section not only because it chronologically comes before many of the other skills but because I consider it more important. If we cannot craft effective problem statements, all the other capabilities will be diluted in their effectiveness.

5

Studying Cause and Effect

Lean is often described as turning all employees into a community of scientists. The perpetual pursuit of knowledge by understanding cause and effect is at the heart of that description. This knowledge is truly a competitive advantage and an asset because you leverage that asset for continued returns over time. The more you understand the cause and effect of your work, whether that is assembling components, closing the financial books, engaging a customer, or writing code, the better you are able to solve problems when things go wrong and make improvements to drive performance.

Without understanding cause and effect, you are often left with "trying stuff" and more randomly finding what works. As we mentioned in chapter 2, trying stuff is essentially how we start solving problems as infants. It is random, chaotic, and unlikely to drive sustainable performance. Organizations that do not seek to understand cause and effect will often rely too much on benchmarking and copying answers from others. With this approach, you can only hope those are the right answers.

Key Elements of This Capability

This is often referred to as the scientific method, and all the things that go into the scientific method for the advancement of knowledge of science should also go to the advancement of knowledge in your own work. Problem solving becomes the pathway to explore that knowledge, and problem statements from the previous chapter describe the vector required to gain knowledge.

This description, from *The Map of Knowledge* by Violet Moller,[6] describes some of the core elements as well as demonstrating how ancient these practices are: "Euclid, Galen, and Ptolemy pioneered the practice of science based on observation, experimentation, accuracy, intellectual rigor and clear communication—the cornerstones of what is now known as 'scientific method.'"

Observation, mentioned first on this list for a reason, is often central to this practice because you are observing real work at the real point of activity under real conditions. This is the ground truth. In *The Hitchhiker's Guide to Lean*, we referred to this as *direct observation of work*. In lean terms, this is often referred to as going to the *gemba*, a Japanese word meaning "real place." It is often used as a reference to a crime scene, a fitting description in terms of problem solving. Reality is what it really is, and observation is how you digest what you see. Observation is the pursuit of knowledge, and so the entire purpose is to learn. This means it matters how you observe, along with putting aside assumptions and biases that affect how you digest your observations. You must get as close to true, unhindered, unfiltered, and unbiased observation as possible for observation to be most effective.

---

6   Violet Moller, *The Map of Knowledge: How Classical Ideas Were Lost and Found: A History in Seven Cities* (London: Picador, 2019), preface.

YOU MUST GET AS CLOSE TO
TRUE, UNHINDERED,
UNFILTERED, AND UNBIASED
OBSERVATION FOR IT TO BE
EFFECTIVE

It helps when observing—and in general, when digesting any sort of information intake—to do so through an organizing filter. We will later briefly explore tools that help you apply this skill, but the point is that there is a method of organizing all you observe. If you sit on your front porch watching the world go by, you might look at different forms of transportation, from driving to flying to walking to biking, or you might digest what you see by natural and human-made, or by color, or by their purpose. The point is, information that is not organized rarely leads to useful insight, and so you must organize your observations to help drive the needed insights for problem solving.

This is also part of the rigor mentioned above in reference to the ancient scientists. As it relates to problem solving, a useful perspective on rigor is to gather a bit more information than you actually require. You are seeking knowledge, and therefore the rigor is about gathering knowledge through the practice of problem solving. This knowledge will serve you well, especially when you get to those inevitable moments of failed solutions. In product development, a helpful analogy to this is testing to specification versus testing to failure. If you test your product to specification, you need only answer the question: Will it work as intended? If you test the same product to its failure point, you gain knowledge about the entire operating range possible, and that knowledge will be useful in the next design cycle or in this one if something fails. This is the rigorous pursuit of knowledge that must take us past the minimum effort required.

The Pursuit of Knowledge in Problem Solving

All problem solving, when done well, is about the pursuit of knowledge. If you already knew what you needed to know, then you would just execute the solution. Problem solving is about closing your knowledge gap before you can close your performance gap.

Most problem-solving templates and models have this pursuit of knowledge built in. In chapter 2, we described how tools and templates provide value as a job aid to help guide the right actions but do not require that you use them correctly. It might be referred to as understanding the current state or current condition, or possibly finding a root cause. The problem with most, if not all, of these templates is they focus more on a tool or technique and less on the questions that need to be answered. If you have the right skill, you ask the right questions regardless of the tool or template. It begins with two questions. First, what do I not understand about the problem? Second, what is the best method to learn what I need?

The first question might sound obvious, but in practice, it is not. When I am observing problem solving, what I see happen repeatedly is people start writing down all the things they know. After all, what they know is their comfort zone. This is the part of the process where we need to get uncomfortable because we need to identify our knowledge gaps. Some intuition is required to develop these knowledge gaps, and we will explore developing that intuition in chapter 6. To help guide that intuition, there are two types of learning gaps that we can identify.

The first is discrete knowledge. Discrete is where there is an answer, but we do not know it yet. For example, the question of the temperature at which water boils has an answer. The second type is continuous knowledge, and this type never achieves perfect knowledge, either because it is infinitely complex (Why do humans do what they do? or How does the economy work?) or because it is a moving target (What's the best technology for cybersecurity?). It is important to understand what type of knowledge gap you need to close, because it shapes our strategy for gaining knowledge. It also helps avoid the limitless pursuit of knowledge beyond our needs, because if the type of knowledge is continuous, then we need a sense of how much knowledge is good enough.

What is also important to consider, although harder to identify, is not only what knowledge we are missing but what knowledge we currently assume to be true that is wrong. It is nice to move stuff into the "known" bucket, because we can then move on to other things. However, when our knowledge is wrong, our problem solving will fail. It could be wrong either because it was wrong when we originally gathered the knowledge or because things have since changed (which is a more common situation). This is why part of the skill of studying cause and effect is holding knowledge as assumptions to be tested and retested when needed. Knowledge evolves, and we, as problem solvers, must evolve with it.

Closing the Knowledge Gap

Once you understand your knowledge gap, you must determine the right method or approach for closing that gap. Too many problem-solving techniques are too narrow in their approach. I understand that in teaching problem-solving tools, we want to be helpful and guide people in their problem-solving method. In some environments, where many of the problems have a similar nature, this becomes more appropriate. For example, many people who come out of manufacturing know many of their problem-solving efforts are discrete quality failures that have a root cause and so tend to build something like 5 Whys into their problem solving. Recall my story of the 5 Why Downtime Report from chapter 1. This worked because the vast majority of downtime events have a discrete failure. This is appropriate, as it is often helpful, but problem-solving skill goes beyond being led *by* the template; it requires leading problem solving *beyond* the template.

I wish I could give you a menu or algorithm that makes this easier. Again, our intuition, which we cover in the next chapter, helps cultivate this decision. The most important aspect is to make a conscious and purposeful choice about your method, because this makes you prepared for noticing when your selected strategy is not working based on the reason you selected it. Long ago, I was working with a team that had a problem statement about reducing their fines and fees to their customers, mostly the big box retailers. In most of their past efforts, they typically got to the current reality portion of problem solving and did a process map. This was in part because many of their problems in the corporate office were larger, cross-functional processes that needed to be streamlined, and process mapping was an appropriate method. There was no process to map for generating fines and fees, so they set out to map the process for registering and reconciling their fines and fees. It was done through observation and meticulous process mapping.

Their efforts were well-executed. They were then stuck, not knowing where to go next. They had selected the wrong tool and done so either unconsciously or subconsciously and therefore could not recognize why they were not getting useful answers. They were horrified when I told them to throw their map away, but then we started laying out the problem on a fishbone diagram, found five or six areas to dig deeper with direct observation, and within a few months, they cut their fines and fees in half.

If you have a multidimensional problem that is not likely to be a single cause, a fishbone diagram is often a great starting point. However, unless it is in a product or manufacturing environment, I would propose a different framing of the branches than the traditional method. Draw four branches (or bones) of your fishbone for these categories:

- Process and Systems

- Skills and Tools

- Principles and Behavior

- Evaluation and Metrics

This is slightly broader for many complex business or organizational problems and helps you organize as you dig into understanding the problem.

If your problem is complex or has many causes, then causal maps are a great tool to organize your observations. It is still important to observe and gain new knowledge and not just draw a diagram of what you already know. A causal map helps you organize which variables affect other variables. When everything is connected, pulling almost any lever will help your problem, but some levers (or causes) will have greater leverage in making progress on your problem.

If you have a process problem, such as needing to reduce your lead time, then there is no single failure mode but instead many opportunities to help close your gap. This is where process mapping helps. It is extremely helpful to look at all the delays, handoffs, durations, loops, and so on in the process, rather than just trying to find the single biggest time element. The reason is that process design often requires looking at the whole and not just designing around one element. This is especially true when it comes to time, as one element is rarely all that significant. This, of course, depends on the problem statement, because if you need to go only 5 percent faster rather than 50 percent faster, how much you consider redesigning is a factor. As an example, we were looking at a tool and equipment requisition process and wanting it to go faster, as there were a lot of things happening in the process scale-up that required fast action. If we looked at it discretely, we would have found the longest handoff and tried to make it faster. But when we looked at the whole process, we found that batching the approvals in a daily huddle eliminated all but one of the handoffs, dramatically reducing the time it took. We were not just trying to fix a discrete failure—we were rethinking the entire process. This broader understanding of cause and effect is what drove breakthrough improvement.

Process mapping is, in itself, a whole category, as there are many different ways to perform process mapping or value stream mapping. There are so many nuances in these methods that might make one better than the other, but as long as you are seeking an understanding of the current reality of the process, then "good enough" might be fine. All process maps are abstractions of reality, and ultimately, they are a tool to help you have a conversation and gain a common understanding of the current reality. Process maps rarely give you the single right answer, and so it is hard to pick the absolute wrong mapping technique if you treat it right.

Sometimes you do have a discrete failure with a root cause. The 5 Whys technique is one of the most underappreciated tools in problem solving and is particularly useful for those many problems that never get the honor (or burden) of having to be tracked and captured on a tool or template. Even for organizations that use this, I can easily tell the difference between 5 Whys as a skillfully used tool versus being a box on the template. If your template has lines on it for 5 Whys, there is a good chance it is just boxes to fill in. Five is rarely the right number, as it is just an estimate to demonstrate digging past the first couple of whys. Sometimes three is the right answer, and sometimes you need seven whys. In part, the skill is in knowing how deep you must dig.

There are so many more methods. Sometimes you can gain the knowledge you need just by looking it up once you have clearly defined your knowledge gap. Or you learn by asking someone. Or using data science, artificial intelligence, cameras, language processing, interviews, and so on. This book is not meant to be a course on how to use each of those methods. There are plenty of ways to learn them, including Wikipedia. The skill to develop is not just in how to use them but in making the right decision about what method to select.

Finally, an important part of the skill of studying cause and effect is to validate the knowledge you have gained. You might talk with people, observe, or run an experiment to test whether you have got it right. As a simple example, imagine your television remote control does not work. You think it is the batteries, but you are out of batteries. Before you run to the store, certain that you are right, you might take batteries from something else and test to see whether your guess is correct. If it is, then you go to the store. If your hunch is incorrect, then you go back and figure out what knowledge you are still missing. This is the approach of a learner, continuously searching for an understanding of cause and effect.

6

Integrating Intuition

There is no logical way to the discovery of these elemental laws. There is only the way of intuition, which is helped by a feeling for the order lying behind the appearance." Striving to make the point of this chapter clear, I am leading off with this quote by none other than physicist and problem solver Albert Einstein. Perhaps the problems he was struggling with do not seem to relate to the problem solving many of us deal with day-to-day, but it is all discovery of cause and effect, and intuition has a very real role. The "order lying behind the appearance" is where the logic and analytical side of problem solving come into play, made much stronger by the pursuit of understanding cause and effect, which we explored in the previous chapter.

It is the integration of intuition and creativity along with the logic and analytical thinking of structured problem solving that makes problem solving most effective. Staying in the realm of physics, Max Planck, the father of quantum physics, said, "Again and again the imaginary plan on which one attempts to build up order breaks down, and then we must try another. This imaginative vision and faith in the ultimate success are indispensable. The pure rationalist has no place here."

To clarify, we will separate troubleshooting from problem solving. Troubleshooting is solving the same problem over again. Troubleshooting is knowing how to jump a car battery or changing the right setting on a computer. The solution is already known, and we just have to match the condition to the solution. Problem solving is about discovery. It is a problem that we don't yet know how to solve, and therefore it is an act of discovery, not just solution matching.

WHO KNOWS THE ANSWER TO THE PROBLEM?

PROBLEM SOLVING IS TO BE USED ON A PROBLEM WE DON'T KNOW YET HOW TO SOLVE. IT IS AN ACT OF DISCOVERY, NOT JUST MATCHING

TROUBLESHOOTING   PROBLEM SOLVING

What Is Intuition?

There are two ways I like to describe intuition and the role it plays in problem solving. First, do this experiment. Seriously, stand up now and try this. Stand on one leg. Can you do it? You probably can. Your body naturally interprets inputs and makes small decisions about how to adjust to find an equilibrium. Next, try to think your way through your balance. Tell your leg to shift left or roll right or jerk forward. Now pick yourself up off the floor, get a bag of ice for whatever you hurt, and understand the experiment. Your active brain is not the only way a human being learns. When you get out of your brain's way and let it do its job unencumbered, it is amazing what it can accomplish.

Second, intuition is still about science. It is still about understanding cause and effect. It is still about how the world works. But it is knowledge that we are within reach of but have not yet codified. We do not yet have the math for it, or the model to explain it, or the evidence to discover it. But it is real. Our intuition is telling us so. This part of intuition is very much built on the study of cause and effect and the rigorous and continuous pursuit of knowledge from chapter 5. Through that pursuit, our intuition is built and utilized throughout future problem-solving efforts.

Problem Solving Is Active Thinking

Thinking, Fast and Slow is a fascinating book by Nobel Laureate Daniel Kahneman.[7] He describes our thinking as System 1 and System 2. While these are not the most descriptive names, the difference is critical. System 1 is fast and often driven by emotion. System 1 is how we get through the day living on existing knowledge without having to expend energy and time thinking through tasks. We decide what to eat, what to wear, and even what to do next in a very rapid fashion without needing process, tools, standards, or criteria. We just act.

System 2 is very different and distinctly human. It is slower, more deliberate, and more logical. System 1 might be how we troubleshoot, but System 2 is how we often should solve problems. Much of problem

---

7   Daniel Kahneman, *Thinking, Fast and Slow* (New York: Farrar, Straus and Giroux, 2011), part I.

solving is designed to slow us down and engage System 2. We are actively managing *how* we think about the situation—in this case, a problem.

The first step of integrating intuition is knowing when we should engage System 2, or when to engage in active thinking. There is nothing that tells us this or forces us to engage our active thinking, because we can deal with most things identified as problems in System 1. Distinguishing when to break from routine and solve the problem is a critical decision. In the last section of this book, The Role of the Leader, we will explore how to make this more systematic, but at the individual level, we are particularly dependent on our intuition for this decision. The more time we spend in System 2 solving problems, the stronger our intuition becomes about when to shift into that mode.

As Daniel Kahneman writes on the subject:

We have all heard such stories of expert intuition: the chess master who walks past a street game and announces, "White mates in three," without stopping, or the physician who makes a complex diagnosis after a single glance at a patient. Expert intuition strikes us as magical, but it is not. Indeed, each of us performs feats of intuitive expertise many times each day. Most of us are pitch-perfect in detecting anger in the first word of a telephone call, recognize as we enter a room that we were the subject of the conversation, and quickly react to subtle signs that the driver of the car in the next lane is dangerous. Our everyday intuitive abilities are no less marvelous than the striking insights of an experienced firefighter or physician—only more common. The psychology of accurate intuition involves no magic. Perhaps the best short statement of it is by the great Herbert Simon, who studied chess masters and showed that after thousands of hours of practice, they come to see the pieces on the board differently from the rest of us. You can feel Simon's impatience with the mythologizing of expert intuition when he writes: "The situation has provided a cue; this cue has given the expert access to information stored in memory, and the information provides the answer. Intuition is nothing more and nothing less than recognition."

We are not born with intuition, but it is built by working in System 2 in a deliberate and learning-oriented way. Working in System 2 is enhanced through the testing and learning we will describe in chapter 8, as well as broader reflection on your problem-solving practice.

Leveraging Intuition in Problem Solving

Leveraging intuition is not about discarding logic, methodology, or analytical thinking. It is about integrating it, balancing the two capabilities. As Carl Sagan wrote:

It seems to me what is called for is an exquisite balance between the two conflicting needs: the most skeptical scrutiny of all hypotheses that are served up to us and at the same time a great openness to new ideas. Obviously these two modes of thought are in some tension. But if you are able to exercise only one of these modes, whichever one it is, you're in deep trouble.[8]

Put a different way, from author Madeleine L'Engle, "Your intuition and your intellect should be working together ... making love." This point is that it is not just about having intuition but integrating intuition along with your logical, structured problem solving.

On a practical level, there are a great many decisions that are made throughout problem solving that are rarely based entirely on logic and analytics. Examine how you generate your initial problem statements. You might be faced with solving the problem of why a defect occurred or instead why you didn't detect the defect when it did occur.

---

8   Carl Sagan, "The Burden of Skepticism," *Skeptical Inquirer,* 12, no. 1, Fall 1987.

Which problem do you decide to solve? If you are faced with not scoring enough goals as a soccer team and want to break down the problem, do you look at the type of shot, the positions, the time of the match, the location on the field, or something else? There are so many choices, and you do not have time to analyze all of them. When considering the scope of the problem, do you deal with how two teams collaborate or instead how you accommodate the lack of collaboration? You cannot test everything. You cannot analyze everything. These are examples of critical decisions for your problem-solving approach, yet these are decisions usually made from or at least guided by intuition.

Leveraging intuition is less about deciding when to use it than about allowing the space for intuition to insert itself in the process when needed. William Beveridge, in *The Art of Scientific Investigation*, building on the work of John Dewey, shared this perspective:

It is not possible deliberately to create ideas or to control their creation when a difficulty stimulates the mind, suggested solutions just automatically spring into the consciousness. The variety and quality of the suggestions are functions of how well prepared our mind is by past experience and education pertinent to the particular problem. What we can do deliberately is to prepare our minds in this way, voluntarily direct our thoughts to a certain problem, hold attention on that problem and appraise the various suggestions thrown up by the subconscious mind. The intellectual element in thinking is, Dewey says, what we do with the suggestions after they arise.[9]

This means the key method to leverage is allowing or creating space. Space allows both the conscious and subconscious minds to work together. Although this is a personal practice, and related to

---

9   William I. Beveridge, *The Art of Scientific Investigation* (Caldwell, New Jersey: The Blackburn Press, 2004).

problems I am working on alone, I take a long walk or even a swim and avoid music and podcasts to just think about the problem. I do not always return with an answer, but I always make progress on how to approach the problem.

Within a more collaborative setting, this means knowing when to create space. Pushing through and continuing to work is not always productive, and allowing time for members to think, or soak, on the problem will help engage their individual and collective intuition.

Allowing detours from the prescribed process can be productive. It allows the team to engage different parts of their mind and forces them out of the linear thought process. Problem solving should be nonlinear, iterative, and even loopy. Create those elements in your work to allow more space for intuition to be leveraged.

Developing Intuition

As already mentioned, one of the key ways to develop intuition is an active pursuit of the knowledge of cause and effect, which we covered in chapter 5, along with working in System 2 to develop and cultivate your understanding. This is not just about the problem; it is about problem solving itself. You want intuition about *how* to solve problems. To do that, you cannot just take a tool off the shelf, follow it as dogma, and plow through problem after problem. This is why we spent time in chapters 1 and 2 framing where problem-solving tools help and how they can hinder. You must develop your own intuition through testing new and different approaches, experimenting with how you solve problems, and perhaps most importantly, active reflection on what is and is not working in your problem-solving efforts.

Develop your own knowledge about problem solving. Even better, do it collectively with those you collaborate with, and your shared intuition will grow through trying new things, experimenting with your approach, and reflection. The best problem-solving organizations might have first learned how to solve problems from other companies, but they ultimately developed their own approach. The pursuit of that approach develops great knowledge about how to solve problems throughout the organization.

Problem solving does rely on analytical and logical thinking. It relies on data and experimentation. But without the integration of intuition and creative thinking, we will always be stuck in our current mental models and perspectives on the problem. Problem solving requires the integration of intuition with analytical thinking.

7

Ideating and Selecting Solutions

If you have effectively framed the problem and clearly understand cause and effect, you are well on your way to solving it. However, you still need a solution. Most problem-solving training surprisingly brushes past this challenge. That it is in part because it is fundamentally difficult to teach, particularly as it's not procedural. There are no step-by-step directions. Yet, without a solution, then no problem is solved.

Ideating (or Brainstorming)

In the later chapter on Creativity over Capital, we will explore the importance of the volume of ideas and brainstorming. Brainstorming is a term for "organized ideation." I actually prefer the term "ideating" or "ideation" because while brainstorming might convey more about how the team works, ideation relates more to what the work is all about. According to the Free Dictionary, the actual definition of ideation is "to form an idea, imagine or conceive."

It is worth understanding why the volume of the ideas generated is so valuable. It is the pathway to creativity. If you generate nine different ideas, there is a good chance the first three are the obvious answers. The next three are the impossible answers that just need to be said, worked through, and ultimately dismissed. Occasionally, in that batch, you will find you wrongly assumed it was impossible. The final three, usually after a pause and even some frustration, are the creative solutions. Why is this?

There are many reasons, but the most important is that your brain can only process so much simultaneously. You must give voice to the solutions bouncing around in your head, whether stupid ideas or not, in order to make room for more ideas. Get them out of there, write them down, speak them to others, do whatever you need to so your brain can move on from that idea. Give your brain space to breathe. This, in part, engages the intuition we explored in the previous chapter.

Another reason volume makes a difference is that some of those obvious or impossible ideas generate more ideas, either because you iterate off one of them or combine a couple of them. Sometimes what makes them impossible is that they just go too far, but if you trim a little off the impossible idea, all of a sudden you see it could work. This is the art of subtraction, where taking away aspects from an idea makes it strong, but it can only be done when you have a starting point to subtract from.

A long time ago, I was a design engineer for the drivetrain of the Plymouth Prowler. The Prowler is a retro-styled production car modeled after many hot rods. The Prowler has a unique drivetrain configuration, and no previously used method of connecting the engine and transmission would work. We developed many ideas and looked at how others had solved similar challenges. None of those ideas would work, but by taking a couple of variables away from an impossible solution (which I tested, blowing up a test stand in the process), I ended with a unique design that worked.

A final reason for volume and pushing through the other ideas is that I have often found the creative ideas were actually achieved earlier in the process, but the people who had them did not want to give their ideas a voice. This is because they thought the ideas might be stupid, they were not confident enough to speak, or they figured if the ideas were good, someone would have already had them. But once you start to hear other crazy and impossible ideas, then throwing your idea onto the pile doesn't seem so hard. Then the person finds out their idea is actually brilliant.

Tapping Creativity

You cannot just turn on creativity, but you can stoke it. You can encourage it, guide it, push it, but ultimately, it must be allowed to happen. There are many books trying to teach us how to be creative when developing solutions. Yet, while often inspiring, they fall short of codifying how to unlock creativity. Alas, there is no method that always just works. It takes practice. It takes experience. It takes the intuition described in the previous chapter. Creativity is a muscle that you can build through practice. Practice is the most important aspect for the development of creativity. What is great about creativity practice is that, unlike some other skills, it does not always have to be purposeful. For example, I practice my strategic creativity by building a new business idea, in relatively significant detail, every single month. I have no intention of following through on most of the ideas, but it still helps me keep my creative muscles toned.

Here are a couple of other tips to get you started. Look for similar problems in different situations. What is the key aspect of your problem? Is it about time, space, force, or preventing errors? Once you have isolated what is most important about the problem, look for similar situations where that aspect has been solved. In particular, look to nature. The natural world has many creative solutions and, of course, never violates the laws of physics, so you know its solutions are at least feasible. How does the shape of a spider web help your problem? How do trees forming rings help your problem? How does the symbiotic relationship between clownfish and sea anemones help your problem? It is amazing how some of these solutions might illuminate ways you could solve your problem, even if you cannot copy them.

Another trick is to think, "What would _____ do?" Of course, you need to fill in the blank yourself. Maybe it is a person you know who operates a certain way. Or maybe it is an organization. If you are working on a logistics problem, maybe you would ask, "What would Amazon do?" If you are working on a customer experience problem, maybe ask, "What would Chick-fil-A do?" You might not solve it the same way, but the potential solution might be exposed. And regardless, you have had an opportunity to exercise your creativity muscle, which is never wasted effort.

Leverage the Lean Rules

The H. Kent Bowen and Steven Spear article "Decoding the DNA of the Toyota Production System"[10] helped frame lean thinking by defining four rules. The first three provide guidance about how to look for solutions, and the fourth will be the main topic of the next chapter. The first three rules describe how we should be thinking about solutions and can provide guidance about what good solutions look like. I have found different language useful for application (in comparison to how they are described in the article). The first three rules are as follows:

1. Structure every *activity*

2. Clearly *connect* every customer and supplier

3. Specify and simplify every *flow* path

These three rules describe an ideal state condition for any process design work. When used properly, they can help stoke your ideation. For example, if your problem is an activity problem, then you ask yourself, "How can I structure the activity to produce the result I want?" Or if a connection, "How can I clearly connect this customer and supplier pair?" Or "How can I simplify or specify this flow path?" These questions do not give you an answer; you must still come up with the actual solution design. These rules narrow your focus and frame the solution space. We are fundamentally more creative when we are working with constraints. These rules help

---

10   Steven Spear and H. Kent Bowen, "Decoding the DNA of the Toyota Production System," *Harvard Business Review*, September–October 1999, https://hbr.org/1999/09/decoding-the-dna-of-the-toyota-production-system.

provide some structure to what good process-oriented ideas will look like. They are used not just to help find problems but also to develop solutions.

Invite Conflict

Too often, we are taught that we should avoid conflict when brainstorming. Certainly, there is a time and place to put aside conflict. However, conflict is one of the forces that helps drive creativity. Conflict should be introduced, productively, by inviting exploration into the disagreement.

WECOME CONFLICT!

CONFLICT IS ONE OF THE FORCES THAT HELPS CREATIVITY. IT SHOULD BE INTRODUCED, AS LONG AS IT IS PRODUCTIVE, BY INVITING EXPLORATION INTO THE DISAGREEMENT

Examine why there is a disagreement. Why do you think my idea will not work? Listen to a critique of the idea. It is important to get into the detailed nuance. "That won't work," and "We can't do that," are not useful criticisms. Even if they are correct assertions, they do not advance the thinking. Getting into the details of the criticism can lead to breakthroughs. First, there are often assumptions, perspectives, or facts behind those comments that help us better understand cause and effect, or something about the environment in which the solution must exist. Second, it can often be found that most of a good idea is discarded only because of one element. Figure out what that element is and fix it, and the rest of the idea suddenly becomes brilliant. This is where productive, collaborative conflict can push things forward.

Creativity requires energy. Conflict can provide a bit of discomfort that gives people a little extra push. It can still be safe conflict. But without the energy, we may not expect to see people push themselves out of their comfort zone. This can be a delicate balance. Too much conflict, and people will disengage. Not enough conflict, and we stick with safe solutions. Invite conflict into your ideation process but manage it.

If working on a problem by yourself, you can still do this. Give yourself some challenges. Set a goal of how many solutions to come up with in a certain time, and a little tension will be brought into your process. You can also invite someone into your process with the sole purpose of challenging you, poking holes in your ideas, and pushing you to develop them further.

Selecting the Solution

If you develop multiple potential solutions, you, of course, must select one to implement. Most people make a critical mistake in this process. They figure out how they will decide *after* the potential solutions are developed. The reason this can be such a big flaw is that any decision about how you will select a solution has clear consequences about which solution you select. For example, if one person says, "We should pick the least expensive solution," and another says, "We should pick the fastest solution," then we might as well just say, "I propose option A." This makes it exceedingly difficult to avoid bringing bias, assumptions, and emotion into the decision process.

I propose that the method, usually in the form of criteria, be determined much earlier in the process. It does not have to be complicated, but if you get these criteria established early in the process, then you can relax. Focus first on generating ideas and then use the selection criteria to make a decision.

The easiest way to have a method determined early is to make it a standard. Some organizations have a set of criteria, usually presented as some form of decision matrix, such as a Pugh chart, that is used for all problems. This has some pros and cons. Having a standard is easier. The task is done, and so there is one less thing to worry about. The second benefit is that it provides some consistency in decision-making across the organization. For example, if everyone is choosing the frugal solution, then that pattern creates a true outcome across many solutions developed. Without such consistency, if some groups are choosing the deepest but most expensive solutions and others the quickest and cheapest solutions, they could be working against each other.

The downside of a standard is that you cannot put your own situational spin on the selection. Context in problem solving is local and situational. Each problem might have its own nuance, and tailoring to those details may help. It also provides a great coaching and learning moment for the people owning the problem. You learn more by developing your own criteria. Find the right path for your organization. My preference is to start with a standard for ease and consistency but then to give individuals and teams the opportunity to add or subtract as they feel it is appropriate.

Sometimes organizations do really well with essentially a single-variable standard. For example, always pick the solution that is best for the customer, or always pick the simplest solution. There is a lot to be said for simplicity. We sometimes convince ourselves that we have done more and better work because we made it complex. But if we choose the simplest solution, there are a lot fewer things that can go wrong during implementation.

There is one criterion that should always be a part of selection. That criterion is: we have tested it. Sometimes you can test multiple solutions and make that a part of your selection process, and sometimes your selection is only temporary until you test it. Either way, this is a vital part of selection, and we will cover it more in the next chapter.

8

Test to Learn

Most problem solving happens either on paper, which doesn't actually change anything, or inside our head, which is fraught with dangers of bias and emotion. In the end, all those efforts must ultimately meet the true judge: reality.

This is where testing comes in. Testing and experimenting are engaging purposefully with the real environment in order to learn. It is not a step as much as a skill, and here's why.

Test throughout, Not Just at the End

Testing is something we should be doing throughout the problem-solving process, not just at the end. Many people mistakenly believe this is something you do only to verify your solution works. That is a useful aspect of testing but definitely not the only place you should do it. Testing is how you answer the question, How do you know? That is a question you should be asking yourself throughout problem solving.

Imagine you are working on understanding the current state and the root cause of a failure. You do a 5 Whys exercise and get to a theoretical root cause. You feel good and are ready to move on. But you did the 5 Whys in the space between your ears and on the sheet of paper. How do you know you are right? Depending on your confidence (which we'll come to next), you might want to test to learn.

Imagine you are trying to figure out why your outdoor lights are turning off. You do your analysis, and you believe that the morning dew has enough moisture to cause a trip in the circuit. That certainly makes sense, but are you sure? How could you test that your root cause is valid? Well, how about you take a spray bottle and squirt water on certain weak points in the circuit to see if it trips? If it doesn't trip, you may not have found the root cause. If the solution is no more work than doing the experiment, then this test might not be that useful. But if the solution was to rewire, then it would be a very worthwhile test.

You test to learn at any point where you want more understanding. Test throughout the problem-solving process to validate knowledge, not just to validate solutions. Test to learn.

What Is Your Confidence?

There really is no such thing as certain knowledge, only degrees of confidence. At one point, we knew the earth was flat, that leeches cure disease, and that there were nine planets in the solar system. Consider what we think we know today that isn't true. As we are testing, we need to take into consideration both what we are trying to answer and how confident we need to be.

What we are trying to answer depends very much on what we have confidence in and what we do not. We might need to verify only that the solution will work. We may have more confidence that it will solve the problem than we do that it will work, and so we only need to test that it will work.

We may not be sure it will solve the problem, so our testing must verify that. Or we know it will solve the problem, but we are not confident under what conditions. Will it robustly solve the problem under all conditions? Can we test for that? Of course, those tests would be far more extensive and expensive, and this is why we have to be clear about what questions we need to answer.

We also need to understand what our confidence depends on and how important it is to test versus moving forward without a real test. Testing takes time, effort, intention, and sometimes money. Therefore, we should approach our testing strategy with purpose.

First, how much effort we expend on testing should depend on how important it is to get it right. Will it affect public safety? Employee safety? Customer satisfaction? Or will it just be frustrating and obvious to us if we get it wrong? Some learning is worth more effort in validation than others.

Next, consider the complexity of the testing environment. The more complex and the harder it is to get good data and validation, the more important it is to understand the environment. If you are going to test and end up not really learning anything, then it probably isn't worth the effort. Finally, consider the ability to actually perform the test. Sometimes you can test only the solution but cannot test that it solves the problem. As an example, most of the TSA (Transportation Security Administration, the US's airport security agency) is designed to prevent things such as airplane hijacking. However, when changing procedure, you can't validate the result based on whether there is, or is not, a hijacking. But TSA can test whether their procedures are able to catch someone trying to bring a gun through the airport (unfortunately, some reports suggest they fail this test the vast majority of the time).

Consider these factors in your testing strategy, because it is a game of inches. A little more learning, a little more validation, a little more confidence, backed by good use of testing, will provide you with the most knowledge for your efforts.

Fast and Cheap Tests

The most important variable in testing is that they are valid. The test conditions should represent, as closely as possible, the real conditions that the test must relate to.

Beyond that, we want to make our experiments as fast and cheap as possible. Now, I hate the word cheap, so we can say inexpensive, whether that be resources or money, but "fast and cheap" is still a pretty clear guideline.

The key is that you do not want to invest more resources into your test than you would lose by being wrong in your implementation of a solution. The cheaper and faster you can experiment, then the faster and more you can learn from your testing efforts.

As an example, a company that builds websites for large companies used the same practices others follow. They would design the website, build it, and then bring in focus groups to test and validate the outcome. But at that point, they were nearly done, so if there were information that suggested they should start over, no one was likely to consider that new knowledge because too much has already been invested. They changed their approach to designing websites on paper, drawing pictures of different layouts and features. They would do focus groups rapidly just by putting drawings of websites in front of people, watching their eyes, and asking them what they would do next. They were able to test a much broader range of solutions much faster and ultimately learn a lot more at a much lower cost before investing their dollars in development.

In another example, we were working in a factory that had to recycle a great number of large steel barrels. The recycled barrels were deposited into three large truck-containers. Because there was no natural discipline about which container to deposit the barrels in, too frequently, all three containers would fill simultaneously, and they would have to call for an urgent pickup at a higher fee. The potential solution was to put clear signs in front of two of the containers, forcing people to fill up only one at a time. Many good permanent solutions were proposed. They decided to do a test, which was basically to put a handwritten cardboard sign on a broomstick and stick it in an orange traffic cone. It worked. This solution didn't work in all conditions because the signs would deteriorate in the rain and the cones would tip over in the wind, but they now knew it worked and could proceed with a permanent solution.

Test Your Hypothesis

Testing is not really about validating your idea. Testing is truly about validating knowledge. You have studied the current reality and should have a model (even if in your head) of how things work. This model represents your knowledge. Is it right? How you perform your test can help tell you.

The key step is the development of a hypothesis. I do not really care if you use the word "hypothesis." However, what results do you expect to observe when you make the change you are planning? This key step is making such a declaration. It helps you validate your model of how things actually work. And I propose that the knowledge gained and validated is far more valuable than just knowing whether a solution worked or not.

THIS SHOULD WORK NOW... LET'S TEST IT

TESTING IS ABOUT VALIDATING KNOWLEDGE. THE KNOWLEDGE GAINED BY VALIDATING YOUR MODEL IS FAR MORE VALUABLE THAN JUST KNOWING IF A SOLUTION WORKED OR NOT

I was giving a speech at a conference years ago, and right before me was a top professional poker player (during the time when there were at least five different poker television shows). I don't play poker, but I understand the basics of the game. He told me knowledge was essential. Especially early in a game, if he thought someone was holding a pair of queens and he couldn't possibly beat them, he would still call the bet. Why would he spend money if he knew he would lose? Because he thought he could read the player and the situation, and spending a little money by losing a hand was a small price to pay to validate whether he was accurately reading the situation or not. This is an example of an individual who understands the value of knowledge.

Testing is about knowledge. Problem solving is ultimately a knowledge game. The more you test your knowledge in a deliberate way, the more your problem solving will be effective over time. This is the game of problem solving we have all come to play.

SECTION 3

Problem-Solving Culture

Peter Drucker famously stated, "Culture eats strategy for breakfast," making quite clear its importance in the hierarchy of building better organizations. This is true for problem solving as well. In the first section, What Is the Problem with Problem Solving?, we established that the tools are not the distinguishing factor in problem-solving success. The second section, People-Centered Capabilities, got us off the page of the problem-solving templates to understand how the capabilities of people move problem solving forward, with knowledge and learning being central themes. Yet as evidence proves time and time again, no matter how talented a team can be, the wrong behaviors will ruin them. In this section, Problem-Solving Culture, we examine key behaviors that define excellence. The six behaviors described in this section will start within the process of problem solving and grow in perspective to the ecosystem in which problem solving occurs.

9

Learn Deliberately

As lean grew in popularity through the 1990s and 2000s, there was one commonly accepted truth: lean was, above all other things, about waste elimination. This was productive and fruitful, but to me, felt wrong. I always believed lean was more about problem solving than waste elimination, and while I stand by that statement, it isn't quite right either. The reason problem solving is so central to lean is because, when done properly, it gets directly at what lean is really all about. Lean is about *learning*.

This became very clear to me as I was equally involved in two growing communities, lean and organizational learning, the latter made popular by Peter Senge's *The Fifth Discipline*.[11] At the time, my employer, Chrysler, was quite involved in teaching the learning organization, and I became an instructor (among many other roles). But much of organizational learning, while creating a mindset of being open to learning, did relatively little to create deliberate learning. This was when I started to become perhaps the first strong advocate for the idea that lean is the best strategy to actually build organizational learning, and problem solving is the best method.

Deep Observation

One of the most powerful demonstrations of the behavior of learning within problem solving is the act of deep observation. Deep observation is also referred to as "going to the gemba" or often just "gemba," where *gemba* is a term referring to the "real place." Going to the point of activity is a great start, but it is what you do there that matters. While we mentioned it as part of the capability of studying cause and effect, it is the behavior surrounding it that makes it so powerful. Deep observation is the act of seeking an understanding of the systems of work, whether that is technical, process, or even the customer you serve.

In *The Hitchhiker's Guide to Lean*, we referred to this as *direct observation*. "Direct" essentially referred to the same idea as the *gemba*. Deep observation involves more than just being at the point of activity. It requires that you try to look past your assumptions and stories to seek new insights. You must suspend your assumptions, and this is the hardest part. It requires some confidence that what you can learn

11   Peter M. Senge, *The Fifth Discipline: The Art & Practice of the Learning Organization*, 2nd ed. (New York: Random House Business, 2006).

is more powerful than looking like you already knew what mattered. It requires that you ask questions (even if they are just of yourself), primarily about *why* the work is the way it is. That is what makes deep observation all learning; you seek to understand the *why*.

When I started my lean learning journey, I was responsible at Harley-Davidson for the pull system that was put in place (as I mentioned in chapter 1). The system was not working, and I spent most of my time firefighting. By the end of the week, there would be a full day's worth of production sitting around, mostly waiting for parts that weren't available when they were assembled. We brought in resources each weekend to clean up the repairs and then on each Monday started building bad bikes again. I put down my radio, stopped chasing parts, stepped away from the desk, and spent two weeks doing nothing but deep observation. My boss, who would walk the length of the building on the outside so he didn't have to talk to people, thought he knew the answer. He also thought my two weeks were being spent designing the details of his solution. I needed to approach this observation with the purpose of learning. I didn't stop the problems or mistakes that I saw, but each time I asked why. These whys were systemic, both in the system design and, more important, in the mindset of the people operating that system. We set to work on fixing the behaviors and produced an 80 percent improvement in materials-related line stoppages.

The Power behind the Capabilities

In section 2, we covered five specific problem-solving capabilities. How you *think* about those capabilities, however, is more than just the skill and experience with which you apply them. It is about the spirit and about the underlying belief that problem solving is all about learning.

Chapter 4 was about Creating Problem Statements. That seems pretty straightforward, although even as just a skill, hopefully I demonstrated it is not as straightforward as you think. But does learning apply when you are deploying this capability? Absolutely, and here is how. Most people assume the problem statement is obvious, and the goal is to get through the task. But instead, be curious about what you are assuming and what could be true. You should hold the problem statement lightly. I recommended in that chapter that if you do not know the gap in performance, you should write: "It is currently X and needs to be Y." You have documented for all to see that you do not know and have to learn about the gap. Many people I coach understand my point but fail to write the problem statement in this way because it is more comfortable to write a problem statement that doesn't expose our need to learn. Even good problem-statement development can be approached with a behavior of deliberate learning.

Chapter 5, Studying Cause and Effect, and chapter 8, Test to Learn, are obviously all about learning, and so I don't feel the need to elaborate any further. Chapter 6 on Integrating Intuition is not quite as obvious. The utilization of intuition in problem solving is not as much about learning, but the cultivation of intuition requires deliberate learning practice. A favorite perspective of mine is that experience is not what you have been through, but it is what you take away from your experience that counts. This requires active reflection, which helps activate the learning within your intuition.

As a soccer coach, I look for any chance to learn and cultivate my intuition. If I sit down to watch a match on television, I do not usually just sit and passively watch. I will put myself in the shoes of one of the coaches, focusing either on the whole team or just one line, such as the defensive or midfield line. It is important not just to watch what happens but anticipate and predict. In other words, develop a hypothesis. Then I get to compare what happens to my knowledge and then test that knowledge. This is deliberate learning, which is much more productive than passive learning.

Useful Knowledge Connects Cause and Effect

In chapter 7, we explored Bowen and Spear's article, "Decoding the DNA of the Toyota Production System," and their phrase "community of scientists" to explain Toyota's environment. This is an excellent description of this behavior. Plenty of people know what works for certain situations. We know resetting a breaker might fix the electrical outlet that doesn't work, we know our days are longer in the summer, and we know a smartphone can access the internet from almost anywhere. Scientists must understand why those things are true, at least in their chosen domain of study. They must understand what causes the effect they are observing.

This pursuit of understanding cause and effect is true in a lean environment, but the domain is the work you and your team do. A lean thinker must understand *why*, even when they do not have a problem to solve. When they do have a problem to solve, they must understand both why the problem exists and why the solution works. This is cause and effect. "It just works" does not get the job done. The "try stuff" problem solving we learn as infants does not make us a deliberate learner but an accidental one. This is why many strong lean organizations do less benchmarking than other companies, because much of benchmarking results in copying solutions without understanding the why behind them. When a lean-cultured organization does benchmark, it has a more focused learning objective and a deeper study to ensure that the cause and effect are understood.

This behavior of deliberate learning is valid at any level of work. It applies to strategic questions, such as "Why does our customer prefer our baseline model more than our premium one?" It applies to workflow problems, such as understanding "Why does our process take thirty percent longer than our customer's required response time?" And it applies to personal work issues. As an example, a recent question for me was "Why does my ability to achieve my primary objective vary from day to day?" I started deeply observing my personal workflow and my accomplishment of tasks from high to low priority. I made several small changes to my work, but perhaps the most significant was that I reordered the tabs on my browser so that in the morning, I first looked at my calendar to see what I had that day, then looked at my personal kanban board (a method to organize your work) to see what tasks I had laid out, and only then did I look at my inbox. This was not a tip or trick I pulled off the internet. It was generated from understanding my problem and my work and fundamentally understanding cause and effect. It was an exercise in deliberate learning.

Problem Solving Is an Investment in Knowledge

As I stated at the beginning of this chapter, I believe problem solving is the most powerful element of lean because its true purpose is to help people learn. Investing time and energy into problem solving is an investment in knowledge. Removing or resolving problems results in improved performance today. Solving problems properly results in improved performance today but also builds knowledge for tomorrow.

This long-term view is often a hallmark of effective lean cultures—understanding what we can do today that will lead to long-term and sustainable performance, even if that investment is hard or time consuming (see section 4 on Success through Coaching for more examples). Investment in knowledge is powerful for two primary reasons.

First, knowledge built today leads to speed in the future to innovate, create, solve, or otherwise take ownership over your performance. The better you understand your process, your work, and your cause and effect, the greater number of safe risks you can take to purposefully try new things to enhance your performance or rapidly resolve breakdowns in your performance. Knowledge is one of the few sustainable competitive advantages because, when done right, you keep building it. If you open up a big gap with your competitors and continue to invest in building knowledge, they can never catch you.

Second, knowledge allows you to dig into finer granularity through detail and nuance in your work. The phrase "The devil is in the details" refers to the details being mysterious to someone, and that mystery leads to undesired outcomes. The phrase was actually an allusion to the phrase "God is in the detail," which means anything worth doing is worth doing thoroughly—as in, the details matter.

This is one reason many strong lean cultures are often slow to invest in new technologies (other than the ones they innovate to deliver value for the customer) and abhor "black boxes" of solutions that might seem to work. They cannot observe or understand why, and this is more important to them than the benefits of an off-the-shelf solution.

A Daily Choice between Learner and Knower

As with most lean behaviors, this is not a choice between a good person and a bad person or a lean person and a traditional person. The choice is between a learning act and a traditional act, or a learning behavior and a traditional behavior. That choice must be made repeatedly, and it is just a matter of how often we make the right choice.

What is the choice between an act of being a learner and an act of being a knower? A learner seeks to engage with a problem with deep observation, curiosity, and openness. They develop a hypothesis they can test. That test isn't for approval or disapproval, but is an experiment meant to drive learning. That hypothesis might be: "If I take this left turn on my daily drive home, I expect to save ten minutes." It is a statement of knowledge of cause (the turn) and effect (the ten minutes). The experiment is to learn more. Putting aside the challenge of how many days I need to collect data for it to be valid, if my experiment demonstrates I have saved ten minutes, then (a) I get to keep my solution because it is effective, but also (b) it validated my model of understanding my system. If I save only five minutes, I will still keep the solution because my performance has improved. Instead of just accepting that, however, a learner will go back and understand why they saved only five minutes instead of ten. They want to understand because that knowledge will be useful in the future, either to solve a new problem (such as a detour) or to make further improvements.

The real test of a learner is whether they achieve fifteen minutes in savings. That is wonderful—they saved more than expected. While probably keeping the solution again, the learner still returns to their knowledge and examines what they do not understand about the current conditions. The knowledge is far more valuable in the long term than the solution.

The knower has a slightly different path. They assume they know what they need to know. Deep observation is not necessary. Jumping over that hard work, they can create a solution they are certain will work because their knowledge tells them it will. And then they implement the solution without testing it. There is no new knowledge gained.

To be clear, this is a perfectly acceptable pathway much of the time. If you are getting wet in the rain, you jump to the solution of opening an umbrella. If you are hungry, you eat something. The learner knows when to make the decision between being a knower and a learner and uses it strategically to build knowledge about their work. Our intuition (from chapter 6) also helps inform us of when to be a learner versus a knower. This builds a community of scientists, and that provides a sustainable competitive advantage of deliberate learning that is nearly impossible to beat.

10

Pursue the Ideal State

Legendary football coach Vince Lombardi declared, "Perfection is not attainable, but if we chase perfection, we can catch excellence." That is at the heart of the behavior of pursuing the ideal state. More important than the definition of that ideal state is the pursuit of it. Of course, where you are heading matters, but when pursued properly, there is flexibility in that pursuit. An organization or individual that adopts the behavior of pursuing the ideal state never stops moving forward under the premise of "good enough." While informed by competition and customers, the motivation to improve is internal, powerfully driven by that pursuit.

The man who brought this term to life was Robert Fritz, author of *The Path of Least Resistance*,[12] although the principle already existed in many high-performing companies, whether articulated or not. The term he coined was "creative tension" and does the best job of defining why the pursuit of the ideal state is so effective.

The first part of that is the tension between the current reality (which we have already explored in the previous chapter and in the

---

12   Robert Fritz, *The Path of Least Resistance: Learning to Become the Creative Force in Your Own Life* (New York: Random House, 1984).

section on capabilities) and the ideal state. I distinguish tension from stress. Stress is knowing you are not where you need to be and you don't know what to do about it. Tension is understanding the current condition and having that vision of the ideal state and the ability to move forward. Stress often impedes action. Tension compels action.

The creative part helps define that action. There are two uncreative ways someone can reduce their tension. First, they can lower their vision: "We don't have to be that good." While not the intention, often benchmarking is an effort to set the bar to the minimum requirement to be competitive. Second, they can raise their perception of the current reality: "We're really not that bad." In either scenario, the tension is reduced, relieving the need to actually make progress. The creative part is about finding a path to actually move closer to that ideal, as that is the only journey worth pursuing.

Ideal State in Problem Solving

The ideal state in problem solving has been elusive. One reason is that many problem-solving methods, at least structurally, move on quickly to solutions or countermeasures after the analysis of the current condition and do not have the development of an ideal state as a deliberate step. Many lean thinkers, especially those who are alumni from companies such as Toyota, would argue that this should always inform the direction of problem solving. However, if a problem-solving tool or template is meant to be a standard or job aid, my contention is we should help people think about this difficult part of the process.

The other reason this is elusive is that it is truly difficult. We do not commonly think in terms of an ideal state. We do not have a lot of practice. We have not built that muscle to think creatively about where we really want our problem or process to end up. Many people struggle with the ideal state because problem solving has mostly been a defined box with a required gap to close and nothing more. Even if it is not a box on a problem-solving template, thinking through and articulating our ideal state is a fundamental behavior within problem solving that must be cultivated and applied.

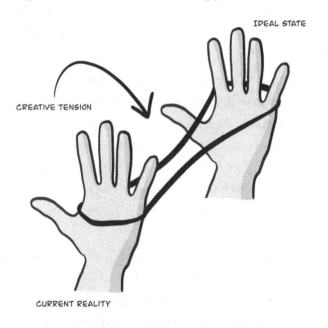

IDEAL STATE

CREATIVE TENSION

CURRENT REALITY

When attempting to think through the ideal state, most people struggle with the difference between the *what* and the *how*. Their ideal state is simply the absence of the problem or perhaps a really good number such as zero defects or 100 percent on-time delivery. This is a good start, as it at least raises the bar beyond standard performance levels. However, this is not very informative in helping set a direction of how to get there.

Another way to distinguish the two elements of *what* and *how* are the target versus the target condition. The target is the *what*. It is the outcome or a result, whether a statement or a number. The target condition is *how* things work in achieving the target. I might have a target weight that I want to achieve. That is a number. But there are many potential *hows* that go along with that. It is not just how to get there but how you operate when in that target condition. You could have surgery, or you could increase your exercise and improve your diet. What does "good" look like when you have achieved your ideal state?

Here is an illustrative example. When working on quality and defects, you uncover that many defects are visible in the work itself, where the defect was created. You set about trying to create an ideal state, and so you write, "Don't pass on defects from your own work." This is a great start. That is what we are ultimately trying to achieve. But how do we achieve it? What does good *look* like? How do you think about the ideal process that delivers that outcome? You have a target but not a target condition.

If you leave it there and move on, a perfectly acceptable solution is to fire anyone who passes on a defect. Wait . . . that's not what you wanted? Then we will try something more positive. Anyone who catches someone else passing on a defect is rewarded with a bounty. Is that not much better? This starts to illustrate that having a target outcome is not enough to create the tension and guide our improvement. What is good about how we work that we are trying to pursue?

Let's try this ideal state: we will clearly and rapidly connect available help to the problem at the point of activity. That starts to paint a picture of how we will operate when we achieve the ideal state. This provides guidance to acceptable solutions. An *andon* process is a method developed within Toyota that allows someone to highlight a problem at the moment they discover it and, with help, contain the problem where it is discovered. The *andon* seen when benchmarking is a neat idea that you can copy. But to ideal state thinking, it looks like a solution that helps us achieve both the *what* and the *how* of our ideal state.

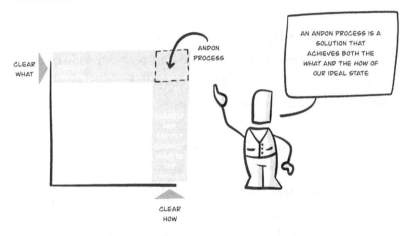

Target Condition versus Ideal State

To be honest, I have personally been very sloppy about interchanging these terms. That has, in part, been on purpose. Many of my clients have their own language, and I prefer to use their language rather than impose my own unless it is a deliberate effort to advance their thinking with language. Also, most of the time, at least for the user, there is little difference, and therefore it can feel like an academic exercise rather than a practical distinction.

However, I feel there is a difference. Theoretically, at least, the ideal state never changes. Our ability to see or envision it might change. We might not be ready to see it, either because it is so far away and seems impossible or we do not have enough experiences that can help shape it and therefore it is too vague. In either case, the true ideal state is not useful to us. So, enough of the theoretical exercise. How does this fit into our daily practice and behavior?

The target state is the next milestone on the way to your ideal state. You pursue the target state, and then reevaluate your progress against your ideal state, and then set another target state, and then reevaluate. That is easy when you think about outcomes. If I want to lose weight, first I lose five pounds, and then ten, and then twenty. But in terms of the how, this is harder work. Because people cannot always envision the ideal state, the next target state is all they can envision, and that is where the lines begin to get blurred. Years ago, at a bank, you wanted faster lines, and then after progress was made, you wanted no lines, and then you wanted remote and digital banking from home.

Here's a simple example. The ideal state might be that we design our work so that "It is impossible for any defects to occur." Zero defects occurring is the outcome, and error proofing to a thorough degree is how we achieve it. But that seems so far away and might not even be helpful to inform the solutions to our problems. So, we establish a target that "No defect, once created, escapes the person performing the work." And if that target state is too elusive, then something closer would be "No defect escapes our team's process."

Here is another example to further illustrate the concept. Later in this book, I paint the picture of an ideal state that every manager is a problem-solving coach to their team. For many reasons, that may sound ideal but might also be so far away from the current condition that it doesn't help us with our next steps. Let's compare two different target conditions. One target condition might be "Every manager can coach on problem statements." An alternative target condition might be that "Twenty percent of director-level managers can coach on problem solving." Both of these target conditions help get us closer to the ideal state, but each shapes different pathways to get there. These are the instances where thinking through the target state can be helpful, but they also show why an ideal state is so vital because we need to know where we are ultimately trying to go.

Countermeasures versus Solutions

As I have already mentioned, I am not uncompromising when it comes to language, so I'm less particular about whether you use the word "solutions" versus "countermeasures" than I am about the behavior that accompanies it. The pursuit of the ideal state means no solution is likely to get us there. Today's solution is simply the best we can do right now until we take further steps or come up with a new idea.

Which word sounds more temporary, "countermeasure" or "solution"? Most people will say countermeasure. What do we desire, a temporary or permanent resolution of our problem? Of course, permanent sounds better, so why do ideal state thinkers often use the term countermeasure? Because for an ideal state thinker, all solutions are temporary. Just because we made the symptom go away or achieved our goal, that does not mean we are done. We might go and work on another problem next and put this one aside. We may never come up with a better solution than the one we just put in place. However, we still see it as temporary. This is just the best we can do at the moment.

This runs contrary to the commonly held principle "If it ain't broke, don't fix it." Those following this principle don't want to mess with something that appears to be working. There are two main ideas that explain the difference. One is that the ideal state thinker is not satisfied with "good enough" and breaks things intentionally to see what they can do to make it even better. If it is not better, then they return to the previous state. The other difference is the idea of understanding cause and effect. If you do not understand your process and your cause and effect, then you are afraid of change because you cannot get it back to its previous level. Effective problem solvers are perfectly okay with meddling and breaking things that are working, because that is how they uncover new ways to get closer to their ideal state.

What Shapes the Ideal State?

When developing the ideal state, what does someone draw on to help shape it? Most of the time, it is informed by the collective experience of problem solving. The more problems you solve in a thoughtful manner, the more your perspective of the ideal state is shaped. So, practice and reflect, and this becomes part of your capability. You are combining both your understanding of cause and effect and your intuition, both explored in previous chapters.

But there is another element that is less often talked about that I would like to highlight. The purpose, or why, of our work should also help inform the ideal state. This is especially true for more strategic problems, rather than a simple defect.

One of the most influential books in my life was Viktor Frankl's *Man's Search for Meaning*.[13] During his traumatic experience in a Nazi concentration camp, Frankl explored his mental state and that of his fellow prisoners. The summary: a person's deepest desire is to find meaning, or purpose, in life. If you find and focus on that meaning, you can survive anything.

A similar conclusion is articulated in the popular book from Simon Sinek, *Start with Why*.[14] Your *why*, or purpose, should inform all your work, including *what* you do and *how* you do it. That *what* and *how* start

---

13   Viktor Frankl, *Man's Search for Meaning* (Boston: Beacon Press, 1959).
14   Simon Sinek, *Start with Why: How Great Leaders Inspire Everyone to Take Action* (New York: Portfolio, 2011).

to sound like an ideal state description, which I articulated earlier. Therefore, your purpose or your *why* should inform your ideal state.

This is true for both organizations and individuals. At Menlo Innovations, a software development company popular with lean thinkers, they have a why: joy. On their website, they state: *Our processes, our culture, our work ethic—they all aim toward a single goal: joy.*[15] This means that any ideal state, whether how to solve a client problem or a work process problem, must be consistent with that purpose.

For me, as an individual example, my purpose has been helping people take control of their own destiny by changing how they think and work. That might not fit neatly on a bumper sticker, but it helps shape my ideal state for much of my work. There have been plenty of opportunities where I could either take on a client project or change how my work is done, but doing so would be inconsistent with that purpose. Clarity of my purpose can be tremendously helpful in my own problem solving.

You might say that purpose is the ultimate ideal state.

---

15   "Our Way," Menlo Innovations, accessed June 30, 2021, https://menloinnovations.com/our-way.

11

Creativity over Capital

Problem solving begins with the problem but must eventually end with a solution. That means we must create solutions, and it matters how we think about generating and deciding on a solution. Of course, skills matter (as we explored in chapter 7, Ideating and Selecting Solutions), experience matters, and effective analysis matters. But if we already knew what to do, then going through problem solving was wasted effort. We do not automatically know what to do, which is why creativity matters. We engage in that solution development with the mindset that we value creativity over capital. We will look at both sides of that equation.

WE KNOW

WE DON'T KNOW

IF WE ALREADY KNOW WHAT TO DO, GOING THROUGH PROBLEM SOLVING IS WASTED EFFORT

Creativity Begets Creativity—Capital Diminishes Capital

Creativity gets stronger the more you use it. That is a tremendous reinforcing loop that problem solvers want to activate. Through disciplined practice, you learn to explore ideas without committing to them, throw away ideas without mourning them, put ideas together without feeling stupid, and evaluate multiple ideas simultaneously without getting lost. Practice is required. Good problem solving often involves breaking down a problem to the smallest possible elements and solving it a piece at a time. This is done because aggregate solutions to aggregated problems rarely work; breaking down the problem is an effectiveness strategy. It also has the added benefit of providing more repetitions, which allows us more opportunities for that practice.

When my eldest son played baseball—a sport that I was never any good at, so I stayed out of any advice or coaching—I would go and watch some of his games. Baseball was a sport where they played a lot of games and generally never practiced. That was fine; it was only meant to be fun. However, he might get two at bats in a game and swing the bat an average of three times each. Sometimes he would produce a hit, sometimes a strikeout or a walk, or, because he stood his ground, more than his fair share of hit by pitches. That produced six opportunities per game to practice, or about twelve a week. If he went to a batting cage, however, he could have sixty repetitions in thirty minutes. A good problem solver is seeking the batting cage of problem solving because it gives more opportunities to swing the bat of creativity. They want repetitions because they want to practice their craft.

Capital works in the opposite way. The more we use our capital, the less of it we have. We can overcome almost any problem by throwing capital at it—people, technology, or other resources. Notice I use the word *overcome*, because rarely are we solving the problem; instead, we are just masking the symptoms with resources. Any company can buy assets and equipment, hire vendors, license technology, or employ people to accomplish their goals. These rarely create sustainable competitive advantages. They create temporary competitive advantages only when spending money is designed to prevent someone else from gaining the advantage, or when they simply do it faster than their competitors. This is defense, which is important if this is how you think about your solution, but it is not a long-term competitive strategy.

Companies produce economic value in large part by spinning out cash; when capital is consumed just to do business and solve problems, an organization diminishes its ability to produce economic value. I have seen several companies who had built up strong strategic cash reserves only to see them eventually disappear once they used them for their strategic purpose (or other rainy-day challenges).

Ideation and Brainstorming

Is this a skill or a behavior? We already talked about ideation as a capability. What does it mean as a behavior?

Whether coaching or doing some kind of review in a boardroom or other setting, I will see someone pitch their concluding solution. One of my favorite questions is, "What was your second-best idea?" There are two reasons I like asking this question. First, sometimes they actually have a better idea that they were afraid to bring up for fear of it being rejected, and we need to hear it. Second, far too often there was not a second idea, let alone a useful second-best idea.

Much of the time, the problem-solving effort was a farce, and the solution was predetermined before the effort was started. But even when that is not the case, this meant there was no rigor, no creative thinking, no ideation behind the solution. This was a choice. The capability is the ability to generate solutions. The behavior is the choice to put that capability to good use. They go together, but you can also have one without the other. I have worked with tremendously creative problem solvers who will engage that capability only when someone facilitates them through a forced process. This is when you get the capability without the behavior.

Again, I am not particular about what words you use. The creator of brainstorming in the late 1930s called it "organized ideation,"[16] but the participants who went through it started calling it brainstorming because they used the brain to "storm the problem." Brainstorming, due to forced and sterile experiences, often has a bad rap. To be clear,

---

16   Alex F. Osborn was an advertising executive. The first of his books to mention organized ideation was *How to Think Up* (1942).

there are many ways to do it. If you sit down and start to write out ideas, you are brainstorming, or ideating, on a solution.

Whether in facilitated brainstorming or individual ideation, the creativity over capital mindset is more focused on ideas than where they came from or how you got there. There are no extra points for originality, only effectiveness. Steal shamelessly. Reapply ideas from other circumstances. Those with a creativity over capital mindset relish the opportunity to apply an existing idea in a new way because they are excited to see how it turns out.

In one case, a team was working on reducing the changeover time of a tool that required pulling a vacuum on the chamber. How could they reduce that time? The capital solution is to buy a more efficient pump. The creative solution stole an age-old solution from the home. If you want to reduce how much water your toilet tank consumes, you stick a brick in the tank to take up some of the volume. Could they do the same thing? They filled the nonoperational spaces of the chamber with small metal blocks, greatly reducing the time to vacuum.

We should also challenge ourselves to see how far creativity over capital can take us. In other words, what can we do that is free? One operation quite often needed a flatbed truck as part of their core process. The truck was not available all the time, and it would get borrowed for all sorts of needs, from a materials pickup to a lunch run. The operation would grind to a halt because the truck was not available at the needed time. The capital-intensive solution was to ... wait for it ... buy another truck. I know you saw that coming, because it is the obvious solution. It also happened to be the impossible solution, because there was no capital available for this group. The creative solution involved greatly reducing the desire to "borrow" the truck for any errand. They painted the truck pink. It could still go on the road when needed, but now it was the very last option anyone would select. And they did not even have to buy pink paint. They mixed some red and white paint they already had. That is the creative solution, and its success inspired the team to many, many more creative solutions on their way to dramatic performance improvement.

The last important thing about having options is what happens when your solution fails. If you have one idea and it looks like it is going to fail or is failing, most people will plow through. We will force it, perhaps dismissing the evidence that it is not working. If you have a plan B, then when the solution does not work, you have a pretty easy pivot available.

Evaluating Ideas

Part of creativity is remaining open-minded to new ideas and new evidence and ultimately finding what works. This is hard because the problem-solving tools can provide cover to make us feel flexible when, in fact, we are not. This cover might take the form of an evaluation matrix, which we described in the Ideating and Selecting Solutions chapter. This is an effective tool to compare different solutions or countermeasures against a set of criteria. Ideally, the criteria are either standardized or set in advance. Otherwise, you start to craft your criteria against your favored solution. If you bring bias into the creative process, the evaluation matrix will not overcome your behavior. Many of the scores are subjective, based on your interpretation of cause and effect. Your bias will naturally skew the evaluation, even if you are not aware you are doing it.

There is one method that is much better at breaking the tie between competing solutions if our biases end up in the evaluation process. That method is experimentation. We discussed this in the Test to

Learn chapter, but it is powerful because it uses the one thing our minds cannot bend: reality. Do lots of experiments, even on the things you think will fail at, because it will lead to more creative ideas and a greater understanding of the problem.

The key to this is experimenting as cheaply, quickly, and easily as possible. There is a concept in the lean startup community called MVP: minimum viable product, a phrase coined by Eric Ries in his book *The Lean Startup*.[17] What is the minimum product I can put out into the world to test the value proposition with a real customer? We should be doing the same thing with our countermeasures. What is the smallest, cheapest, and fastest test I can do to learn about the feasibility and effectiveness of my countermeasure?

This also works with two countermeasures. If we can't agree between solution A and solution B, it is doubtful that further discussion (or argument) in the conference room will yield a result, unless one person just gives up out of frustration. (I doubt those decision criteria ever make it into the presentation.) Test both, learn from them, and see what new ideas emerge from the process.

The one surprising thing that can come of this: sometimes the minimum viable countermeasure is the final solution because it was good enough and it works. As an example, one automaker wanted to develop better solutions for heating and drying the paint on a car. They built a wire frame and attached hair dryers to test different heat profiles. It worked well and was cheaper, and if one hair dryer broke, they could easily replace it. They kept the solution, at least for a while.

In parallel to the development of this book, I was also developing a virtual workshop process that combined synchronous and asynchronous learning, real application, sustainable commitment plans, and

---

17   Eric Ries, *The Lean Startup: How Today's Entrepreneurs Use Continuous Innovation to Create Radically Successful Businesses* (New York: Crown Publishing, 2011), 77.

more. I wanted to develop this process into a multi-month master class that could go deep into the learning. I built an MVP that I first called Study Groups and then called Learning Lab workshops. It turns out clients wanted the MVP more than they wanted my original vision because it was more flexible and easier to target and allowed them to take a step, and then another, and then another. I scrapped my own product vision in favor of the test MVP and am dozens of iterations into delivering this product to clients.

The lesson is that creativity involves testing because testing makes us smarter and avoids us getting stuck. So, ideate, compare, test, and repeat as many times as possible, and your creativity will become an asset to drive your problem solving.

12

Collaborate

Problem solving is a team sport. In fact, it is a team contact sport. If people solve problems, then how people work together through and around problem solving is essential to consider. Problem solving is one of the most collaborative opportunities in the toolbox because it often requires collaboration, and we usually have a facilitator to force it.

Solving a Problem Is Its Own Reward

There are no extra points for solving a problem all by yourself. This is true on a grander scale as well. The "self-made man" is a myth. Even some of the most storied entrepreneurs would have never made it without key partners. Where would Bill Gates be without Steve Ballmer? Or Steve Jobs without Steve Wozniak? Or Sergey Brin without Larry Page and Eric Schmidt? Or either of the last two examples without their coach, Bill Campbell? We will return to coaching in the next section of the book. On a large scale, success is not diminished when it is shared. In problem solving, that is true as well. The successful closing of a gap is its own reward, and whether you need one person or twenty people to help does not really matter if they help close the gap.

In most organizations, the lowest number of people who can be involved in a problem is one. People can solve problems in isolation, or even often in secret, all the time. In a true problem-solving culture, the lowest number is two. No problem should be left in the hands of just one person. That does not mean you all have the same role, or equal responsibility, or that every task is shared, but others are indeed involved.

Two Views Are Better than One

Two views are better than one. I don't mean that in a cute "Everyone gets to play" bumper-sticker way. I mean it from a purely practical stance that you need more than one viewpoint to solve most problems. Many of the problems we face in organizations, at least those higher up on the priority list, are experienced by different people, and different functions, in different ways. Two people view the same problem differently. But those views are two things. First, they are valid because they are based on their experience. Second, they are incomplete because they are *only* based on their experience. Of course, sometimes someone's view is just plain wrong, but the risk of this rare occurrence is outweighed by the benefit of leveraging our multiple viewpoints to see the problem more as a whole.

That is the point of collaboration. It is not to ensure buy-in down the road, although that is certainly a benefit. It is to make us *smarter* about the whole of the problem. If I am facing you and start drawing a clockwise circle with my finger, what do you see? You see a counterclockwise circle. We could argue indefinitely about whose view is correct. Someone might come out on top—not because they were right but because they had more power or persistence or were simply louder (a tactic that sadly produces results, albeit not progress). That is no way to understand a problem. Only by combining our two (or more) views do we see the picture more as a whole.

I remember watching teams of technicians and engineers work together on improving preventive maintenance procedures. The engineers saw the equipment and what needed to be done. The technicians saw the execution of the work and how to best and most efficiently deliver it. For years, they solved the problem independently and unsuccessfully, leading to variation, downtime, quality problems, frustration, and animosity. When they started working together, they saw the problems more as a whole from both perspectives. Standards were built, problems solved, and both the results and relationships improved.

"They" Are Not the Enemy

So much problem solving treats the other person, the other team, or the other function (collectively referred to as "they") as the enemy. "They" are preventing me from having success. "They" are creating waste for me. "They" are making my work harder. "They" are the cause of the defect. This makes collaboration much more difficult and, therefore, problem-solving success much more difficult.

The enemy is the waste, or the problem, or the burden, or the defect. We are allies in that particular battle and end up being far more effective when we collaborate to achieve a shared goal. The shared goal is important. When we collaborate to reshape the problem statement to be a shared problem statement, it feels like we are negotiating or sacrificing. When done properly, however, it is not a negotiation. It is adding new information to get to a better, more accurate, and more informative problem statement that is more likely to lead to real success.

There is a bit of psychology here in how we think about another group or person, and the problem. When we come face-to-face with someone without either the structure or the mindset of problem solving, it is a debate, a discussion, or a negotiation. That is because the other group or person is our focus and therefore must be part of the problem. When we use a structured approach, whether on a piece of paper or a whiteboard, then that becomes the focus. We are on the same side, working together, and our "debate" is with the problem.

DEBATE   COLLABORATE

This difference is really demonstrated in how different teams or functions engage in problem solving when the problem crosses over organizational boundaries. The traditional and common approach is that one function—we will call them Department A—finds a problem that involves Department B. Whether due to a lack of trust or alignment between the two departments or an altruistic-sounding "We don't want to bother them," Department A gets to work on the problem. They do a really good job, working hard and going deliberately through each step, documenting it in the standard template along the way, and they reach a conclusion on the solution that should be implemented. Proud of their thoughtful analysis and armed with an A3 report showing their work, they present the findings to Department B. Department B now has two choices: accept the recommendation or reject it. If they reject it, it may very well be just because they were not included. It could also be that there is something missing in the problem statement, analysis, potential solutions, or evaluation criteria that means the effort was even a little wrong. If they accept it, they may just accept a solution that is also missing something in its analysis so the solution will be less effective. Finally, beyond the potential harm done to the problem-solving effort itself, Department B is left wondering why they were included only at the end, which is likely to erode trust rather than build it.

A much more effective approach is that when Department A finds the problem, they bring the issue, not yet fully formed into a problem statement, to Department B, and then they work through the process from crafting the problem statement to testing the solution in a collaborative way. Only in this case do you ensure that each step incorporates the right perspective, data, needs, constraints, etc., that are required for a shared solution.

There are several failure modes with the traditional approach beyond those I have already outlined. For starters, because you are working in isolation, it is unlikely you can test your answer, so you select only your solution. When you collaborate, you have a much higher probability of testing potential solutions.

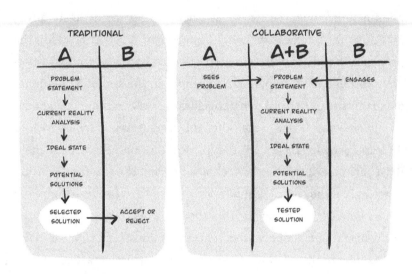

Also, you may not be aligned on whether the problem you observed is even seen as a problem. I remember working with one team on their problem-solving effort. Their effort was complete, but they couldn't get their idea accepted and they wanted to go back through the whole process to see where they made a mistake. We walked through their work, and it was very well done. At the end, I asked, "Does the other person agree that this problem statement is a problem?" The answer was no. They agreed that the problem statement did exist as a condition but not that it was a problem. There was no alignment on the very first step. There was no path forward from there.

Don't Collaborate

This brings me to a final point about collaboration: sometimes do not collaborate. There are two parts to this. First, collaboration is about the process, direction, inputs, and conclusions. Collaboration is not about every piece of work that must be done. Too often I observe an organization fall into routines where every step of the work done to solve the problem involves setting up a full team meeting, which then probably starts to fall into a one-hour-per-week routine. Not everyone is equally committed or available, and the whole thing can grind to a halt. Not every step needs the same level of collaboration.

Collaboration is about involvement and shared interests. It is about gathering the right input, data, and perspectives. It is not about sharing the workload. That is a separate decision with separate criteria. If you took ownership of the problem and engaged another person for input on the problem statement, the approach to understanding the current state, the conclusions of the current state, the ideal state criteria, a brainstormed list of ideas, and how to organize the test of a selected solution, then you have involved that person in a collaborative way. If they did not have the capacity, capability, or simply the interest to go as deep as you did, then that should not prevent you from making progress. This first point is that collaboration on problem solving does not necessarily translate into collaboration on all the work.

The next level of this point involves not collaborating at all. Imagine a situation where you begin to surface a problem and this problem easily makes a "top five" on your list of priorities. You do the right thing and engage the other function that would be involved in solving this problem. They agree that your observation is valid and that it is a problem. You have a great start. However, this problem falls somewhere lower than one hundredth on their priority list. To be fair, the more alignment created of either the ideal state or even the metrics that exist across the organization, the less often this happens, but it will often happen to some degree. What is your choice? This being a low priority is not based on their lack of understanding of the problem but simply about where it falls on their list compared to other gaps.

A common example of this falls between an external customer and as you as a supplier. You might be aligned in a lot of ways and have a long-standing and strategic relationship. However, your customer continues to send surprises your way in the form of new orders that weren't forecasted or planned for. You might be able to do amazing things if you worked on this together, building a solution where you have greater insights into their data and market and they better understand how orders are fulfilled. Unfortunately, they are very busy, and this just isn't a high priority for them. So, your problem statement that focused on variation and late additions to demand will go unresolved.

If you recognize that collaboration will not happen, then you can reshape the problem statement. You assume their part you included in the original problem statement is now out of scope. Your new problem statement is now focused on the impact on your team from that variation and late additions. You accept the input as the normal condition and work hard on the impact it has. Will the potential solutions be as powerful as those a collaborative problem-solving effort would have yielded? It doesn't matter, because rather than being a victim when collaboration is not possible, you still took ownership and accountability over the problem and moved forward.

Collaboration is not a tool. If it requires a facilitator every time you collaborate, then you do not have a collaborative culture yet. Facilitation is a work-around to the gap. Collaboration is not a check-the-box step either. You cannot say, "I met with them," and therefore you were collaborative. Collaboration is how you approach the person or the team and how you approach the problem. Get the collaboration behavior right, and problem solving will yield great results.

13

Initiative and Ownership

Problems do not solve themselves. Systems do not solve problems. People solve problems. This requires that people, in the face of many other pressures, take the initiative and ownership to push through and solve those problems.

We begin by defining these two terms in the context of problem solving. Initiative is about both starting and moving the work forward. Most problem-solving training begins with what you do *after* you have decided to start. The transition from being aware of a problem to starting to actively solve the problem is a larger chasm than many recognize. There are all sorts of barriers in the way to starting: confidence, permission (real or perceived), issues with alignment, and other problems. And throughout the problem-solving effort, new distractions, pressures, and even new problems will surface that can lead to the abandonment of the effort. Initiative is what carries the problem solving forward to success.

Ownership is about your relationship to the problem. Whether ownership is individual, or the collective of a team, or a partnership between two parties, ownership is about taking responsibility for the problem. Owning it means you take on the accountability and responsibility for the existence of the problem and its resolution. This is the opposite of a victim mentality. There is no pointing the finger of blame. Ownership does not mean you will never transfer the problem to someone else; it should be owned by the right person. That begins with who discovers the problem and does not pass it by, but that doesn't mean that is where the problem stays. A culture of ownership will avoid the situation where everyone stands around "admiring" the problem but no one is willing to pick it up.

Prioritizing Time

Initiative means you find a way to make progress, and this begins with the prioritization of time. Of course, no one can "make time." There are twenty-four hours in a day, and although you can choose to spend more of them at work, you will not actually create time. Therefore, what remains is how you prioritize your time, as well as how efficiently you consume it.

When someone claims they do not have time for something, that is hardly ever the whole truth. What it really means is they do not value that activity highly enough to prioritize it in their daily flow of work. It means we *choose* not to spend time on it because we have chosen to spend time on other endeavors. It may not feel like you have made the decision. It could be your decision, or it may be a decision that was made for you. Most often, it results from decisions made long ago that have now become your habits of what is prioritized and what you quietly tell yourself is more important or nonnegotiable.

When you get this behavior right, then problem solving becomes a priority. Other items on your calendar make room for problem solving. You know problem solving is what keeps the organization's performance stable and drives improvement, and therefore it must make progress. This is well done organizationally when you proactively make room on your collective calendars for problem solving. This can take many forms.

Many organizations create standard time for problem solving and improvement in their daily or weekly cadence of meetings. This means other meetings cannot take place at those times. This might be at site level, at team level, or sometimes even at company level. Sometimes this is just a generic block of time, and for others, it is a reserved block after a standing performance-oriented meeting so any problems identified in the meeting can receive immediate attention from the appropriate people.

This serves two purposes. First, it signals in a clear way to the organization that problem solving is a priority. It is regularly on the schedule (just like metrics reviews, budget reviews, and other such meetings), and therefore it is at least as important. This signal helps to shape the culture, and, in contrast to where problem solving is not on anyone's schedule, the signal is quite strong in reverse. Second, it ensures the people you need to collaborate with in order to solve the problem are available at the same time as you. There is no coordination of schedules required because they are pre-coordinated: this is problem-solving time.

In one automotive manufacturing facility I was assessing in Shenyang, China, there was a standing block of time at 2:00–3:00 p.m. every single day. You went to the floor (where the problems were found) at the designated location, with multiple meetings happening across the site. You first reviewed new problems. Then you either started solving new problems or continued to work on existing ones. If you were not needed at that time, you could leave. The initiative of problem solving was, at a minimum, a daily cadence. We will explore more decisions such as this that help shape the culture in the last section of the book, The Role of the Leader.

Prioritizing What to Finish

In addition to prioritizing your time, there is an aspect to grabbing the initiative about what problem to prioritize. Taking the initiative goes hand in hand with prioritizing what to finish. Unfocused individuals, and organizations, hop around from problem to problem, always starting to explore new ones but too infrequently driving existing ones to a conclusion. Half-finished problem-solving efforts have not yet provided benefits. It is more valuable to prioritize what to finish in contrast to prioritizing what to start.

There are three benefits gained from prioritizing what to finish. First, we solve problems to improve our performance. Time to resolution may be one of the most useful metrics of your problem-solving effort. It measures not only the effectiveness but also the urgency, which is driven by the initiative to finish. The sooner the gap is eliminated, or the gain realized, the more benefit we receive from our problem-solving efforts.

Second, we gain learning faster. Problem solving is a learned skill, and like most skills, the more we practice, the stronger we grow. That skill is only strengthened through full repetitions, and that means we must finish our problem-solving effort to build our skill.

Third, the longer our problem-solving effort continues, the more bad habits can creep in. This includes scope creep, the introduction of assumptions, lack of rigor, loss of alignment, and even the inefficiency of personnel changes. These can affect the efficiency of solving the problem at a minimum and can also ultimately affect the effectiveness as well.

Ownership

Regardless of your role and whether you are sitting in a meeting or walking through an operation, you happen to identify a problem. Now

what? This is one of my favorite questions to help assess an organization, both its culture and its systems: When you experience a problem
or observe some waste, what do you do? The answer will tell you a lot
about your culture of ownership.

This begins with the idea of "Find a problem; fix a problem." The
person who initially best understands a problem is the person who
found it. We want that person to be compelled to act. Of course, if we
build effective systems, then acting is much easier. If we build a good
culture, then acting is not treated as an act of aggression, as it can
sometimes be perceived in some organizations.

This is a harder aspect of culture than you might expect. You
probably look in the mirror and believe you will act. Here is an example
of how hard it is. I was teaching waste identification and elimination
to a factory leadership team. We then went on a waste walk. Because
the factory was a clean room environment, we all had to get gowned
up, and that started with a swish of water to clear any particulate from
the mouth. The garbage can was in front of the water cooler, and so
this entire management team danced around each other trying to get
a swig and then throw away their used cups. They even commented
that it was a waste of motion, so they had successfully identified the
waste. They then proceeded onward. After some discussion as to
why, they all admitted to assuming it was someone else's problem.
None of them was universally in charge of garbage can locations.
As a result, even though they together represented virtually all the
decision-making power in the facility, none of them felt empowered
to solve the problem. This is exactly why this behavior is so difficult.

Exposing problems can often feel like you are insulting those
around you because, after all, they did not see the problem. Perhaps
they had made a mistake. Perhaps they had done it intentionally and

were wrong. Exposing the problem can feel like an insult to your peers or your boss. This is just as bad as the other alternative: that you are wrong. Maybe you just do not understand how things are supposed to work. Maybe you had a lapse of capability, and the problem is more an exposure of you than of a bad process. Maybe everyone sees it already, and you are just repeating what everyone else already knows. These are all equally scary reasons for someone to avoid raising a problem.

This is why effective problem-solving cultures depend on a version of *ownership* such as "Find a problem; fix a problem." It begins with: whoever sees it must own it, at least through exposure. That is the minimum expectation. If the worst case is that you learn it truly is not a problem, then, in fact, you learned something and supported the desired behavior of the organization. The best case is that you exposed a problem no one saw, and perhaps it was caught while it was still a small problem.

Ownership does not have to be about seeing it through to completion. The culture of "Don't bring me problems; bring me solutions" is an absolute failure of leadership, yet I often hear versions of it. This will guarantee you hear only about the problems that are easily solved by someone else. You will not hear about problems that are difficult to solve. You will not hear about problems that you must solve. Sometimes the ownership of a problem must change hands. That might happen vertically, with the problem passed on to the boss or further up the chain of command. The handoff also might happen horizontally to another team or function. However, you must own it until a full handoff is complete. This is how to ensure problems do not fall through the cracks.

The final observation you can make surrounds problems that go away on their own. If your team is late in its delivery, then this is a problem. If a team working in parallel is even later than your team, then no one may notice your problem or care about it. What do you do then? Do you convince yourself it is not really a problem because it didn't cause a negative outcome? Or do you highlight and engage with the problem until it is resolved and won't repeat itself? The latter is how you know you have a culture of problem ownership. Tools and templates don't solve problems. People must take the initiative and ownership for problems to get solved.

14

Transparency, Vulnerability, and Trust

As your team and organization learn to solve problems, creating an environment that values transparency, vulnerability, and trust becomes increasingly important. These three words intertwine with each other. It is difficult to tear them apart and explore them completely independently. We begin with some quick definitions as it applies to problem solving.

Transparency is about being visible about the fact you have problems, what they are, and ultimately, what you are doing about it. The phrase "Don't air our dirty laundry" is thrown away; everyone has "dirty laundry," otherwise known as problems, and we are ultimately more effective when we expose them.

Vulnerability is about having what is called a "weakness orientation." We do not project that we have no problems but instead that we are open to hearing and learning about them. If we have nine successes and one miss, we focus on the miss and how we can improve it. This becomes a source of learning and improvement, openness to tough feedback, being shown problems, and metrics exposing our gaps, and so on helps us stay vulnerable and open to enable improvement.

Trust can help enable or destroy both transparency and vulnerability. Trust is a foundation on which we can expose our problems and collaborate openly because we know the spirit with which these behaviors are adopted. Trust in leaders, trust in each other, and even trust in the process all help enable an effective and vibrant problem-solving culture.

TRANSPARENCY IS ABOUT BEING VISIBLE ABOUT THE FACT YOU HAVE PROBLEMS, WHAT THEY ARE, AND ULTIMATELY WHAT YOU ARE DOING ABOUT THEM

TRUST CAN HELP ENABLE OR DESTROY TRANSPARENCY AND VULNERABILITY

VULNERABILITY IS ALSO ABOUT HAVING WHAT'S CALLED "WEAKNESS ORIENTATION." WE DON'T PROJECT THAT WE HAVE NO PROBLEMS, BUT WE ARE OPEN TO THEM

TRANSPARENCY   TRUST   VULNERABILITY

Early Visibility into Problems

Behaviorally, we want and, in fact, welcome early exposure of problems in our work and our processes. Why? Problems exist whether we know it or not. Problems exist whether we expose them or not. If you woke up on a Tuesday morning and went into work and there were no problems to speak of, is it more likely that there are no problems or that you just don't know about them yet? It is almost always the latter. There may not be any crises, but we do not want to wait until our problems become crises.

This transparency should extend into our team and beyond into our team's key relationships. Essentially, there should not be "two sets of books" when it comes to our performance and our problems.

Our personal or internal understanding is the same as our external view. A good test of this is whether you have "pre-meetings" with your team before you are then exposed to a larger audience. Many of these pre-meetings are about getting our story straight, determining our negotiating parameters, and deciding what to share and what not to share. This helps you have a polished and sound story going into the meeting, but it also means you have two versions: the internal version and the shared external version. This is not transparency.

Why is early visibility into problems so valuable? Because that is the best time to fix them. If you believe your process can handle anything, then it will handle anything right up to the point where the problems are so large that they finally break the process. By then, the problem is too large to solve easily or rapidly. This means we actually design our work to be fragile, to break easily, and to help us expose the problems.

Consider building two small bridges over a stream. The first bridge is made from many intertwined twigs, each one easily broken individually but collectively they are strong. The second bridge is made from one much larger, stronger log. If both structures have good integrity, that large, strong log seems better. If there are problems, then the bridge made from twigs will generate its first cracking sound, and before the rest of the structure collapses, you will be able to get to safety or even repair it. But if the log gives way suddenly, with one loud crack you end up hurt and wet in the stream. When you design your process to be fragile, it breaks early but in a small way, and you can fix it quickly while the problems are still small.

Just-in-time pull systems in manufacturing are one example. Inventory between steps is there to absorb problems. When you reduce inventory, small problems will disrupt the flow easily. It does not matter whether the problem is cycle-time variation, downtime, quality defects, or something else. As soon as the problem surfaces, the process will be interrupted. This allows you to respond to the problem quickly and while it is still a small problem.

In a product development team, most controls involve gates, review meetings, and templates. But the important connection in product development is resource-to-resource, such as one engineer trying to integrate a system design with another subsystem engineer. It is difficult to just trust that those two engineers will cooperate and serve one another. We prefer to put more controls in place to maintain the system. Person-to-person is a fragile system. If you build your product development system with enough granularity, you can spot such breakdowns easily. If you also have a mechanism in place for surfacing a problem immediately, you fix small problems quickly before you end up missing a true deadline.

Transparency of Progress

Transparency of progress in solving found problems is just as important. For starters, it answers the question, "Are we working on the problem?" This is useful information for multiple reasons. First, it provides information to management about what is being worked on and what is not. There are a lot of management systems that are designed to review the performance of a team or a process. How much management time is spent trying to determine whether their various teams have a grasp on their problems and, ultimately, on their performance? Transparency can cut through all that overhead.

A good test of this is where performance metrics are presented and whether they have been shared in periodic-based meetings or on process walks. When a metric is presented, is the list of problems identified also included? Too often not. This leaves observers and managers wondering whether the problem is seen, understood, and engaged; if there is a concern, it often leads to interference where it may not be welcome or even helpful.

Horizontally, this transparency is also useful. You may depend on another group making progress on a problem. You may be contributing to that work. It benefits you to know where the work stands. It is equally useful to know whether the problem is not being worked on or will not be worked on. I see so much frustration in organizations when a problem is handed off to another department with the expectation that it will be worked on. It gets put in a queue and then continually deprioritized with no transparency. The feeling on the other side is that it is being done deliberately and with poor intentions. There may have been good intentions, but with the lack of transparency in the deprioritizing of that problem, only the worst is assumed. When you know it will not be solved, you then take ownership and start to solve it from your end, even if the solution will not be as powerful.

For example, if you submit a problem statement to IT for help and they accept it, you are then expecting them to turn around and do something with that problem. However, if you are unlikely to get it prioritized any time in the next couple of years, you might keep the problem statement and find another solution, even if it is not as good as something IT could have done for you. In the end, not only is frustration lower with transparency but more problems actually get solved.

Vulnerability and the Weakness Orientation

The weakness orientation is about being vulnerable to the fact that there are problems. A popular phrase in lean cultures is "No problem is a problem." This means we never assume there are no problems. If there are no problems, then we are not exposing them and open to them, and that is a far bigger problem. Vulnerability is about having the confidence to acknowledge problems because the power is in engaging those problems, not ignoring them.

The thinking that drives this is that any abnormal condition is a problem, not only those that produce noticeable or measurable impacts on outcomes. If a standard is not followed, that is a problem worth solving. If there is not a standard, that is a problem worth solving. If waste is found, that is a problem worth solving. If there is a surprise, that is a problem worth solving. If variation is higher than normal, that is a problem worth solving. These are all opportunities to improve, and the weakness orientation suggests we grab these opportunities once they are visible.

It is critical for this behavior that no energy be expended trying to convince ourselves that everything is fine. That is energy or resources that could have gone into making improvements. I visited one company that had an entire department under the banner of benchmarking, but their sole purpose was to review data and demonstrate that any gaps in performance compared to others could be explained by variables that were outside of their control. Therefore, no action was required. Ultimately, this negatively influenced the culture to one that avoided talking about problems and gaps, and therefore little got solved.

Building Trust as an Enabler

Trust is what enables transparency and vulnerability. Without trust, people are unwilling to be transparent and would rather control what is exposed and what is not exposed. The fear is driven by not knowing how people might use the truth against them. Extending beyond just transparency and vulnerability, trust is crucial for lean success. In recent research I conducted, over 75 percent of respondents indicated trust was essential for lean success, meaning that lean cannot be successful without trust.

Trust also supports other behaviors discussed in this book. Collaboration is greatly enhanced through trust because participants are able to focus on their collective efforts to solve the problem. Without trust, collaboration looks more like negotiation, where the parties involved are either winning or losing as the problem solving progresses.

Learning is also enhanced with trust because "I don't know" is more acceptable and will not be used against someone. If people are less willing to say "I don't know" because of a lack of trust, then problem solving becomes more a demonstration of what we already know instead of what we are learning about the problem through discovery.

Trust is built through four key mechanisms, which I have outlined in previous research and writings. The four enablers are called the 4Cs of Trust:

- Demonstration of *Care,*

- *Communication* of the why,

- *Competence* to deliver on the promise, and

- Doing all these with *Consistency.*

The demonstration of *care* is often first because without a sense on both sides that someone cares, the rest hardly seems to matter. What does this have to do with trust in problem solving? When we are trying to craft the problem statement, the care is about both the problem itself and its impact on people. Without demonstrating care about the problem, it is more difficult for someone to wade into the unknown and work hard in a vulnerable way.

Communication of the why, or context, is also particularly important for problem solving. Why does this problem matter? Who will care if I do or do not solve it? Sometimes within the problem statement, the *why* is incredibly obvious. Often it is not obvious, especially as we start solving more problems that can only be described as abnormal conditions. Why does failing to follow the standard matter? Because it could lead to defects or delays, which would, in turn, lead to deteriorating customer confidence and a loss of sales. The leap from the problem to the "why it matters" is not always easy or obvious, and the more clearly we communicate the why, the easier people can trust in the intention and their efforts.

Competence is particularly important when problem solving involves collaboration. Many collaborative efforts break down when parties do not trust each other's competence. Will you solve it at all? Will you solve it well? Will you solve it quickly? They start taking steps without each other, draw their own conclusions, and do not give each other equal weight in determining solutions. This then ceases to be a collaboration and therefore not a shared solution, which hurts both the creativity and adoption of the solution.

Finally, this must all be done *consistently*. Without consistency, trust in transparency and vulnerability deteriorates with each misstep.

SECTION 4

Success through Coaching

The section following this one will be The Role of the Leader, and I easily could have embedded the topic of coaching into that section and no one would have challenged why I did it. However, coaching as a practice is just as important to problem-solving success as the behaviors and capabilities are, which is why I've committed an entire section just to explore Success through Coaching.

Chapter 15 will outline why coaching is so important, and chapter 16 will explore other key questions of who, when, and where. Chapters 17 and 18 will get into the how and make clear how coaching is truly very different from teaching. Chapter 19 will help you chart a course for building coaches in your own organization.

15

Why Coaching?

Many leadership capabilities can be tied to effective problem solving. Why should the focus be on coaching? What makes coaching so important? I believe this comparison will make it clear. And here is a hint: it is all about your purpose.

When I am coaching a soccer game, often a player is in the wrong position in space. A player should be standing wide, or high, or showing for the ball, or almost anywhere except where they are. One option I have is telling them where they should be. That is efficient. It gets me the result I want quickly. And it signals my true purpose: in that moment, with that act, I am trying to win the match. I am managing the outcome.

Another option is to tell the player where to be and why to be there. Now I have become a teacher. That must be far better, right? It certainly is, but the player is responding to where I want him and why I want him there. It signals my purpose: helping that player know how *I want* him to play. The emphasis is still on me and my knowledge and ideas. It is my team, my playing style, and my information that I want the player to understand. I am teaching.

Yet another option is for me to ask the player, "Where should you be?" Then the player makes a decision. It might be the right decision, or the wrong decision, or a good decision that is different from the one I would make. But she has made a decision. When that player comes off the field, I can help her evaluate that decision, what other options might have been, and what the consequences may have been for those decisions. I have helped her learn how to think about the game. And in doing so, I also reveal my purpose: to make that player better and smarter *beyond* my direct engagement with her. My wish for her is that I will never see her best game because she has learned how to learn and will continue to evolve as a player beyond my time with her. My perspective is that only in this instance am I truly a coach, because coaching is centered on the other person and helping her self-discover her most important lessons.

Telling is an act. Coaching is making a personal investment in that person you are coaching. It shows you are committed to his success. The essential phrase is: "to his success." A coach is invested in the other person's or the team's success. Therefore, the mindset, approach, and even the tools of a coach are designed to help with *self-discovery* (which we will explain further in chapter 17). What a person discovers for himself, he now owns. Lean is a journey for each individual, one heart and one mind at a time. You can achieve true change only when people take ownership of their behaviors and apply their capabilities when they need them, in the way they need them.

Returning to soccer, I remember one of my all-time favorite moments of being a coach. I was coaching a particularly young team, one that did not have a lot of experience or even knowledge of the game. They were playing a game, and by halftime, I could see there were many things wrong. So many that I did not feel I could provide a useful, focused summary of how to adjust them all. Instead, I assembled the team in an arm-in-arm circle and asked each player to share one thing he was doing well and one thing he was not in the first half. They nailed it, down to what each player needed to change. Their ability to self-evaluate was nowhere near complete, but it had started. And that is when I knew I had truly coached the team.

How will you know when you have truly been a coach?

For coaching soccer, this certainly sounds like a good approach and mindset, and surely you cannot take this exact approach in other scenarios. But why is coaching so important specifically to problem solving?

First, problem solving is dynamic. There is no recipe. There may be some standard tools and methods you can use, but you should not be using those in a linear fashion. You must act, react, and adjust. You must analyze and use intuition (as explored in chapter 6). You must go forward and sometimes back. Unless someone more experienced is going to tell you what to do for each problem, you are going to have to think not only about the problem you are solving but also the approach to solving it. As a coach, getting people to the depth of capability where they can own their processes and their decisions makes problem solving quite dynamic.

Second, problem solving requires countless repetitions to master. This is why coaching problem solving is preferred specifically to teaching problem solving. There are a lot of things you can learn in a classroom. With a little practice built in, you can usually leave the classroom feeling fairly confident that you can then tweak, adjust, and improve. You are at least competent. This is not true of problem solving.

I spent some time over the last few years coaching people while they were also attending a three-week program on lean given by the True Lean organization at the University of Kentucky. This program focuses on teachings from Toyota, taught by Toyota alumni, and while it covers a range of topics, problem solving is certainly the centerpiece. After three weeks in the classroom, including plenty of practice, I always ask students how confident they are in their new problem-solving capabilities. Almost always, they feel less competent than they did before the program, and this is because they have learned how much they did not know. They now have a foundation for their practice, but that is just a jumping-off point. They are now open to learning, but that learning takes iteration and reflection to build mastery of these skills. Working with a coach is the best method for such iteration and reflection. A coach helps you learn based on the cadence of the problem, building on the cadence of the classroom. As a student, the next lesson I really need to learn in problem solving might not expose itself in the next problem I engage with or the one after that. But when that moment comes, I am much more likely to have access to a coach than to be in the classroom learning that specific point at that specific time.

Third, learning problem solving is personal. To explore this point, it is helpful to further contrast coaching versus teaching. Teaching is efficient and consistent. It is efficient because a teacher can line up ten, twenty, or fifty people and get them through a prescribed set of content. It is consistent because it is designed, scripted, and delivered in a way to produce a planned result. These are advantages that teaching has over coaching. However, teaching is based on planned needs, not the individual student's needs. It is also done at the prescribed location and time of the training, not the location and time of the problem-solving occasion. Why is learning problem solving more personal than other topics? Because we have been doing it since we were infants (as we explored the "trying stuff" approach in chapter 1). It is not like going to skydiving or scuba school for the first time, where almost everyone starts at the same point. Every person has different biases, strengths, blind spots, and habits related to problem solving. Therefore, coaching is a much more effective means of helping a person get from where they are to where they need to be.

This last point is worth exploring a little deeper. In the foreword to Art Smalley's book, *Four Types of Problems*,[18] John Shook writes:

Problem solving may be the most fundamental of human activities. We breathe, we eat, we sleep. Breathing and sleeping just happen. Then we get hungry or we might get cold. Those are our first problems to solve—how to find something to eat or how to stay warm. Solving problems is how we learned to think. To be human is, quite literally, to solve problems. How to solve problems effectively is fundamental to the reality of our daily existence.

18   Art Smalley, *Four Types of Problems: From Reactive Troubleshooting to Creative Innovation* (Boston: Lean Enterprise Institute, 2018).

This is why our ability to improve problem solving is so elusive. You have done it for so long that changing it can seem as difficult as learning to write with your nondominant hand. Have you tried it? Almost anyone who has had their hand in a cast has tried it, hated it, struggled with it, and as soon as the cast came off, switched back to their dominant hand. However, when a person loses a hand, he perseveres and learns to write with the other hand. Others learn to write with a prosthetic. In some extreme cases, an individual has learned (or more accurately, taught himself) how to write with his foot. Why do I share this example? Because this is the kind of perseverance and deliberate intent needed for many of us to change how we think about solving problems. Problem solving is so embedded in the human experience that to undo it and then redo it is a massive undertaking. It unquestionably takes more than participating in a one-day workshop to change how you think about problem solving.

Do you want to improve how you solve problems? A starting point is becoming acutely aware of the magnitude of your personal gap and realizing the intensive effort that will be required to close it. It will help if, pardon the expression, you metaphorically cut off your hand. That is, create a way, whether through a coach, a system, or any enforcing mechanism, to force yourself out of your old habits. Thus, you will provide yourself the opportunity to replace old habits with new ones. A coach, in this context, could be better described as a *sherpa*, a helpful guide showing you the way on your personal journey. Each journey is a little different and littered with wrong turns, blind alleys, and dead ends. That *sherpa*, in the form of a coach, helps you reshape how you look at, engage with, and solve problems.

The fourth and final reason coaching is so important for problem solving is that both parties develop strength. To be a teacher for all maturity levels and all conditions of problem solving might require a lifetime to build such strength. But if you develop an effective coaching model, you do not need to have all the answers. In acting as a guide through the coaching process, you learn and grow from the engagement as well.

I have personally benefited from coaching more problems than I have solved because I have been able to observe different approaches, different problems I would not have experienced, and different domains. These experiences have all helped shape and inform my knowledge and capability of problem solving. As a coach, when you immerse yourself in your coachee's problem-solving process, you are almost entirely focused on his thought process, while the coachee's attention is split between the problem itself and the method. For this reason, the problem-solving coach can learn even more than the coachee about *how* to solve problems through this engagement.

There are many elements that can enable problem-solving maturity in an organization. Training makes it better. Common tools make it better. Good data makes it better. But for the reasons outlined in this chapter, it is impossible to build a strong problem-solving organization without a central focus on coaching. Coaching is ultimately the lifeblood of capable problem solvers.

16

The Who, When, and Where of Coaching

Most coaching advice focuses on the *how* of coaching, but the questions of *who*, *when*, and *where* are underestimated in the overall impact on the result. These more subtle parameters determine everything from the relationship to the mood, and, if crafted incorrectly, they can lead to failure, no matter how capable the coach.

The Who (the Coach)

There are two aspects to answer the *who* question, as there are two sides to the relationship. Let me cover the less obvious one first: Are you the right person to be doing the coaching with this person at this time? Sports are filled with these examples. The greatest coaches in history cease to be effective often because they are the wrong coach for that group of players at that time in history. The most effective coaches are focused on the outcomes of the other side of the relationship. As a result, they must be willing to step aside and get someone else to engage in producing a better result.

How do we know when we have reached this point? In my observations, it is not obvious. There are other variables we might point to first. For example, someone might approach me about their difficulty: "He is not open to coaching." My inquiry will often include: "Or is he not open to coaching from you?" This is not meant to be judgmental or hurtful. We just need to consider the question. The reason is usually one of a complex relationship they do not want to muddle. Maybe it is employee–boss, maybe senior–junior, maybe peer–peer. Whatever it is, they perceive that the coaching relationship will either be less effective or it will interfere with the other dimension of the relationship. When we build an entire organization's structure around the idea of the manager as coach, then this ceases to be an issue because it is woven into expectations. But we should not let this get in the way of good outcomes.

This mismatch between coach and coachee is usually apparent either at the very beginning or well down the road into the relationship. At the beginning, if you are struggling to even get things started, then you must ask the question of whether it is a good fit. You do not always need to identify why you are a mismatch, but if you are, then hand off the coaching to someone else. The harder instance is when the relationship worked for a while but is no longer ideal. This usually happens when the coach and the coachee get too comfortable and start to share the same risks and blind spots. This is not a matter of duration. I have had ten-plus-year coaching relationships that remain very effective. It is about the dynamic between the two parties.

In my soccer coaching career, I have stepped down from teams to allow another coach to take over. There is no such thing as the "right" time. You do it either before the effectiveness drops or after it drops. It is best to do it before the effectiveness drops, because then you are still in a position to manage the transition in a productive manner. When I last stepped down from a team, it might have been at the height of my effectiveness, but by choosing that time instead of waiting a few more seasons, I was able to select my successor, leverage my trust, and set up the next steps without losing momentum. The kind of coaching we are talking about in this book is not the same thing as coaching a sports team, but the lesson is the same. Transitioning your coachee to someone else is best done while you are still an effective and trusted coach.

The Who (the Coachee)

A more common problem I see people struggle with is who they should be coaching. Most people in a position to be an effective coach are generous with their coaching, which means they will coach anyone who asks and probably many of those who did not ask. But the problem with this is approach is twofold. First, it is dilutive, and the coach gets spread too thin. If you coach everyone you can, you are probably not making as much progress with all of them that you could be with a few of them. Second, it is not strategic. You are not creating leverage with your time and capability when you try to coach everyone.

Imagine you engage with a team. They ask for your help. They are working together on a problem or maybe on their problem-solving capability in general. They have a team leader. They have someone on the team who asked for your help. And you have the team as a whole who is doing the problem solving. Who do you coach?

To be clear, the only wrong answer is to not have a deliberate answer. If you do not know who you are coaching, then it is impossible to be effective. You could decide you are coaching the leader of the team. Your reason for this is that they will be able to lead the team going forward and their commitment to success and ability to guide the team will be the highest leverage for your coaching. You may instead decide you want to coach the person who asked for your help. You reason that they asked, so that means they are willing to learn. You also believe they have some passion, and that passion will translate into practice, which in turn, will translate into competence. That confidence will be a seed to support the growth of the team. And finally, you might instead decide to coach the team as a whole. Your rationale is they will grow together, supporting each other and building skills as a unit, as ultimately most problem solving is a team activity. These are all good strategies. It is too complex to tell you how to analyze precisely which strategy to choose. But the important message is that you have a strategy for who you are coaching. That strategy is meant to create leverage for long-term growth and success, and it provides a focus for your coaching.

The second part of this is whether you are transparent about your role. I have found there is a tremendous advantage to being fully transparent on who you are coaching and who you are not: "I'm coaching you but only helping your team." This gives you more freedom to do things and say things where you are explicit about being the coach. It also gives you boundaries against going too deep when you are not the coach.

Finally, when you are clear about who you are coaching, then others in the relationship can be utilized in different ways to help your coaching. For example, if you have decided you are coaching the leader, you might find a colleague on the team to be some of your eyes and ears to help you observe the leader. You might allow the team to struggle through something because it provides an opportunity for the leader to learn how to work through that struggle. If you were not deliberate about coaching the leader, you would lose that moment because you would instead jump in and help the team through their struggle.

Whatever your method, be deliberate and strategic about who you are coaching. The ultimate goal is to build the kind of organization where every manager can be a problem-solving coach of their team, which we will explore more in other chapters, but for most organizations, that aspiration is far away. Until then, we have a choice to make about who coaches who.

The When

We will cover this more in the next chapter, but coaching is not a moment; it is a process. You do not just have a single coaching conversation and it is over. I would prefer to call those sessions anything else besides coaching. Coaching is a process.

A key question to coaching is whether to make it cadence-based (such as weekly or monthly), event-based (when this event happens, we talk), or a blend of the two approaches. The advantage of cadence-based coaching is you can manage the standard more easily, ensuring some control over the process. You also have confidence that the coachee will not stray too far because you will make your cadence relevant to the speed of the work and the relative risk of failure.

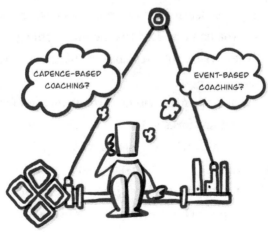

For event-based coaching, you want a defined trigger that will drive the next coaching interaction. If you are cooking in the kitchen, you might let your child get all the ingredients ready and then check to see they got out the right stuff. Then they would mix it, but you would make sure it looks right before it goes into the oven. You know the points of no return, or more likely, where their investment of energy into the wrong pathway is going to increase, and you want to spare them (and you) that waste.

When it comes to problem-solving coaching, in general terms, cadence-based is best for groups and event-based is best for individuals. We'll look more closely at each.

If you are the leader of a team, you will probably have multiple problems being managed by multiple people on your team. You know that sharing the problems across the team will improve both transparency and learning from each other. You may not have the capacity to follow up with every single problem being worked on. You set up a time once a week where the whole team will get together, or at least everybody currently working on a problem. They can share their progress, their questions, and their concerns. You can coach, you can teach, and others can learn from examples. By having a session like this every week, you can rest easy that no one should get more than a week's worth of work off course before you have the opportunity to steer them right.

If you were coaching an individual through their problem-solving process, there are many forks in the road in their work, and the best of event-based coaching will be based on knowing these forks in the road. How do you know the forks? It is somewhat about process but also developing that intuition we explored in chapter 6. Intuition should be integrated into your coaching as well as your problem solving.

As an example of those event triggers, I would love for someone to bring me their first draft of a problem statement. The majority of the time, it will need some work, and since it is the guidepost for all the work that follows, it is best to invest coaching time to get the problem statement well-crafted. This is also a great place to help design a plan for understanding current reality. A great deal of effort is likely to be spent doing this work, and a poor plan will lead to wasted effort. These are great milestones to drive event-based coaching. Define when you want the coachee to return, make sure you are available when they are ready, and then focus on the high-leverage steps in the problem-solving process.

One challenge you may face is that your opportunity to interface with those you are coaching may not match up with either cadence-based or event-based coaching plans. There are always methods around this, ranging from the use of technology to team-based coaching (where multiple coaches work like a tag team). However, if your fit with the needs of the team is too big a challenge, then maybe this is a chance to return to the earlier question: Am I the right person to coach?

The Where

Technology has opened the door for expanding both the *when* and the *where* of coaching, and we have certainly all learned a great deal about that beginning in early 2020. Coaching can be done around the world. I currently have clients in other countries with people I have never met, and we work together very effectively. I have worked with teams where the manager and team members live in separate countries and certain laws prevent them from visiting each other . . . and it works. This has expanded the options of *where,* and we should not be shy about experimenting and leveraging those options, especially where the *who* and *when* take precedent over the decision.

However, there is no question that there is a best place to do coaching, and that is at the point of activity, which we previously referred to as the *gemba*. Of course, this is also the best place to actually perform the problem solving, but why is it so valuable to coaching? Because if you are coaching someone, you do not know what they are capable of seeing and what they are not capable of seeing. When you have the opportunity to stand side by side with someone and you ask them what they are observing in a process and then share what you are observing, it can help build and align capabilities. Once you know someone is observing similar insights to you, you can probably do a lot more coaching from a distance because now it is about sorting what they have observed, not whether or not they observed it.

THE BEST PLACE FOR COACHING IS
AT THE POINT OF ACTIVITY

The *who, when,* and *where* of coaching problem solving do matter, although they probably do not matter as much as *how*, which we will cover in the next two chapters.

17

Coaching through Self-Discovery

The best way for someone to learn is to teach themselves, to discover themselves, and to internalize themselves. If we want lessons to stick, then the more ownership—not just involvement—that the learner has over the learning, the more effective and sustainable it will become. So why do we need coaches?

Even though humans are inherently preprogrammed for learning, it is a messy, unpredictable, inefficient, and ultimately unreliable process when left to its own devices. Our own learning process is filled with flaws. We have confirmation bias, sometimes at incredible levels, that limit the data and feedback we utilize. We do not naturally separate correlation and causation, leading to false and misleading conclusions. We are reactive, learning mostly in response to failure and, after the fact, without a plan to learn. All these built-in flaws in our learning process can lead not only to a slow learning process but also to bad outcomes. If they did not, then humans would learn a narrower set of capabilities with less variation, as other animals do. Our variation of outcomes is part of the source of our ability to create and invent. If our problem solving had as little variation as birds building nests or beavers building dams, we would have fewer failures but also fewer breakthroughs.

Coaching can increase the speed of learning and reduce the error rate while still allowing for, and even encouraging, creativity and self-discovery of learning. This makes coaching one of the best returns on investment in your lean journey. If a new car could get you where you are going faster *and* safer, that is one heck of a combo, and that is what coaching can do for building problem-solving capability. Coaching is your secret weapon.

Coaches Create Experiences

The primary mechanism for coaches is to create experiences. They are inherently designers. Coaches do most of their work, or at least their most important work, without directly engaging with the coachee. If you purposefully create the right experience, then that experience becomes the teacher.

In soccer coaching, there is a phrase one of my instructors used that I have made the centerpiece of my coaching, and that is: "The game is the best teacher." The idea is to let kids play and they will learn a great deal. That does not mean you just play pickup, and it does not mean you don't talk, but the centerpiece of your coaching strategy involves play. And in problem solving, the centerpiece of your coaching strategy must involve the coachee experiencing real problems.

As a brief aside, this is the problem with most problem-solving training. Most problem-solving training involves simulated or crafted problems that aren't real. It needs to be this way for the classroom, for the most part, because it is the only way you can control the flow of the content, the information needed and provided, and even the length of time a step might take. If you said, "Do step five," and it involved three days and a plane trip, you could not really build that into your classroom program. This is why training is much less effective than coaching for problem solving. If you can put the two together, then this is the most powerful method.

Creating experiences for coachees is most effective first and foremost because it is real. You do real work. You solve real problems. This helps learning with nuance because each problem is a little different and with conviction because you are not worried about how the lessons would apply "in the real world" because you are already there.

Creating experiences allows for a combination of learning through success and failure. It is not a prepacked lesson, just a designed experience that allows someone to test, fail, and learn. While we certainly want to learn from failure, having the opportunity to learn from our own success that was not predetermined is quite powerful.

One important point about creating an experience is you do not have to be transparent about what you are doing. Sometimes, the most powerful lessons come when you are not transparent (this is not in contradiction to the transparency we explored in chapter 14 because it is specific within the coaching process). That does not mean you deploy deception but that you have designed the experience without the person knowing what they are supposed to learn. Although a silly example, consider the 1984 movie *The Karate Kid*. Daniel, played by Ralph Macchio, is required to wax the car, sand the floor, paint the fence, and paint the house. He was learning key defensive moves from his *sensei*, or coach, without knowing it (we will return to the risk taken here later). I will do the same thing with my players on the soccer field. We will hold a training session with a series of drills with increasing game realism and decision-making. Sometimes I will tell them the theme at the beginning of practice so they know what I want them to focus on. Sometimes I will not tell them but instead ask them at the end of practice what the theme of practice was. If they can answer correctly, I have designed an effective experience and they have committed to learning from it. These can be my favorite practices.

The last key part of designing experiences is you must help the learning through some form of reflection. This is particularly important for helping coachees develop their intuition (chapter 6). We will explore further how to structure that in the next chapter, but you cannot *only* design the experience. If you let your small kid touch the stove so they learn but do not help make sure they learn the right lesson, it could just as well be "high things hurt" as much as "stoves will burn you." You do not have to tell them the answer, and, in fact, it works best when you don't have to, but you do need to ensure the right lesson is learned through some form of reflection.

Coaches Create Learning Cycles

In order to accomplish learning the right lesson, learning occurs in cycles, and coaches help create those learning cycles. The PDSA, or Plan Do Study Act, cycle provides a fantastic structure for driving these learning cycles (since it is a learning cycle). Before we get into the structure, I want to be clear that you do not need to use PDSA as the structure. If you have another learning cycle you prefer, as long as it maps with the activities I will lay out, then use what works for you.

To start, this is not about one giant PDSA loop to define your coaching relationship. In general terms, the more loops you create, the more learning will occur. The loops will probably fit either into the cadence-based or event-based flow described in the previous chapter. This can be taken to extremes, but I find it is far more likely that there aren't enough learning loops than there are too many. Let me provide a brief breakdown and then apply it more specifically to problem solving.

The *Plan* is you helping the coachee come up with how they plan to approach the task. This could be done through questions, as an assignment, or through something you create together. The point is that they have a plan, which is essential to generate the learning.

Then they *Do* the plan. From a coachee and learning perspective, there is where they are really testing their plan. As I have already mentioned, the best learning comes from real experiences, so this is where the proverbial rubber meets the road.

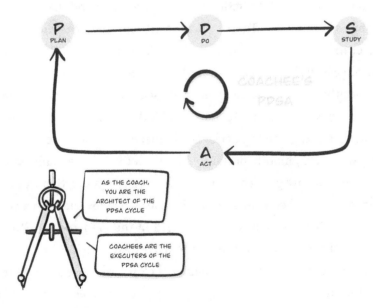

Next comes the *Study.* There is where the coach is helping them reflect on what they learned. These are *their* lessons because it was their plan and their experience in doing the plan. The other steps set up the learning, but this is where it truly occurs and where a good coach can really shine.

Finally comes *Act*, also sometimes referred to as *Adjust*. This is where the lessons from the Study are applied, whether it is going back to the Plan or locking down what is learned in some form of standardization (as discussed in chapter 3).

The term PDCA, or Plan Do Check Act, is used more frequently in the world of lean and continuous improvement. While fundamentally meant to be the same thing, PDCA is often interpreted as a task-oriented loop. Even if it was originally meant as learning, we can all agree that there is more implied learning in the word Study than the word Check. Even Dr. Deming, who used both terms, seemed to prefer PDSA.

That is the basic interaction between the coach and the coachee through self-discovery. To go deeper, we will connect the two different trigger mechanisms from the previous chapter that will determine how you use PDSA in coaching problem solving. Your PDSA coaching will be either event-based or cadence-based. Event-based means you get to the next step, no matter how long it takes, and then we will take the next step together. Cadence-based means we are going to meet every day, week, month, or quarter, and whether you've made progress or not, we are going to work through our PDSA together.

In event-based coaching, you define the next steps and ensure you are engaged. The coach is most engaged in the Plan and the Study steps. In this approach, it is easier to delve deeper into each step of problem solving because the events will map into those steps. Start with the problem statement. We might work through the initial theme of the problem statement and how you would approach developing and getting alignment with the problem statement. That is the Plan step. The coachee would then proceed with that work. When the coachee thinks they have it, we would review both the process and the outcome of their work. That would be the Study step. If you were pretty much on target, the coach would probably allow you to proceed but make some adjustments, and if you were well off target, you would complete the PDSA cycle again for that step with more coaching.

Then we would continue the PDSA cycles through the different phases or steps of problem solving. We would probably have at least two cycles built into the Current Reality phase, first on your approach to understanding current reality and second on your conclusions. Remember the two questions we had in chapter 5 about studying cause and effect? First, what do we not understand about this problem? Second, what is the best approach to learning? We will cover more questions in the next chapter.

We would probably spend one PDSA cycle on the target condition and one on extending that target condition into ideating solutions, which was explored as a capability in chapter 7. Depending on your experience, the coach might not waste any cycles on action planning but focus instead on your verification to ensure you are testing your chosen solution effectively and ensure the testing is driven by learning as we explored in chapter 8. These are event-based triggers and provide a basic outline for coaching problem solving through PDSA.

The other approach is cadence-based coaching. Cadence-based means you have a set interval for interactions with someone. That cadence could be daily or even quarterly (although quarterly is far from ideal). The benefits of engaging on a cadence are that the pattern is easy to maintain and you do not have to worry about someone going too far astray before you have another touch point. They are also sometimes just necessary because there may be travel or other schedule constraints involved in the relationship. The downside is the key moment where coaching might have had the most impact could be missed.

As an example, I used to have a range of clients I would travel to, and because I cannot just hop on a plane when someone completes their problem statement, that means work would be progressed before I showed up. Some visits were every other month and some just quarterly. I could still coach problem solving. The person I was coaching might have completed three problem-solving cycles since my last visit, and therefore I obviously would have missed many potential coaching moments. However, coaching would then focus on the overall approach found across those three efforts or narrow in on certain challenges they faced, and we would set a path for how the coachee would continue his self-discovery cycles before my next visit.

There are pros and cons with both approaches. Sometimes constraints will dictate which approach you take, and sometimes you will be able to determine the optimal solution for the individual and the situation. But as everything in this section has guided you toward, it helps to be deliberate about your choices. In either scenario, you are integrating PDSA as the backbone for creating self-discovering learning.

Coaches Have Their Own Learning Cycles

Coaches learn, too, and this works through what I call Double-loop PDSA. Coaches must have their own PDSA cycle, which is interwoven with the coachee's PDSA cycle but remains their own cycle. This is crucial because every coachee is different and every learning path is different. Your job as the coach is not to teach the coachee the path that you walked but to help them discover the best path for their journey. This is a mistake I frequently observe in coaches in all domains. I will frequently hear another soccer coach say, "This is how I learned it," and, of course, it worked. Otherwise, they would not be a coach today.

That is irrelevant to whether it is best in this moment for this coachee. Every path of self-discovery is a little different. Keep in mind what I mentioned in chapter 15: you are intersecting their problem-solving learning journey that began when they were an infant.

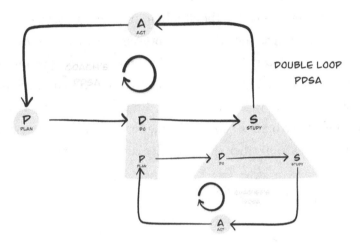

Here is how the PDSA cycles are interwoven. You start with a Plan for your coaching. You hold a coaching conversation with the coachee. That is your Do step, but you are helping them craft their Plan. This is your first connection point between the two PDSA loops.

Then they Do their plan and Study the outcomes. Both steps are ideally also part of the coach's Study step. The coach should be close enough to the coachee that they can observe the actions and approach of the coachee during the coachee's Do step. This helps them evaluate whether the coachee is effectively practicing what they have learned. The coach's and coachee's Study steps are very closely connected. The coach is helping the coachee reflect on their experience but is also learning by evaluating how effectively the coachee is learning and how effective the coach's approach has been. Remember my soccer example where I asked the team at the end of the practice what the theme was? This was my Study step and was feedback on whether the experience was effectively crafted. The coach then uses what was learned in their Study step to modify their approach and return to the next interaction with a Plan.

Coaches must adapt to the situation. They must be learners themselves. Just because something was proven to work in the past does not mean it will work in every situation and with every person going forward. Interweaving their own PDSA cycle with the coachees' is the most effective way to learn together. Ultimately, coaching is a tool for learning. When both the coach and the coachee are equally committed to that learning, then the outcomes can be astounding.

18

Coaching through Questions

Coaching and asking questions go hand in hand. Not many people would be surprised by that. But that does not mean everyone is thoughtful about the questions they ask or how to ask them. Most of this chapter will be committed just to providing examples of the types of questions you can ask during different phases of coaching problem solving, but we first need to spend a little time putting all of this into context.

There are different types of questions, and they are not all of equal value, especially when it comes to coaching. The worst, because it is quite frankly destructive, is advocacy disguised as a question. Lawyers during witness examination are famous for this approach because they are not allowed to make arguments, only ask questions, but they can sneak in an argument. "Isn't it true that ... ?" is a common phrasing. This is sometimes done on purpose, but most of the time, it is done by accident. People might even be convinced they are behaving well because they are asking a question. But if you are truly focused on coaching someone on their problem, advocacy is most often a mistake, especially when it is wrapped in the cloak of coaching.

The next type of question is harmless but also not that useful in coaching. These are simply questions seeking information. "When will the report be ready?" or "How many units are left in inventory?" have no coaching value. They are the simple everyday questions we all use. There is nothing wrong with these questions, but do not confuse them with coaching or leadership questions, as their sole purpose is to collect information.

Then we have two types of questions that are both designed to support learning. The first kind are those questions that help shape someone's path or next steps, and the second type are questions that help someone think and reflect.

What do we need to shape someone's path? Coaching is largely about creating experiences so someone can self-discover the essential lessons. That means we must help shape those experiences so they provide the maximum learning. The right types of questions can help do that. These types of questions help shape the path like breadcrumbs, helping them think through the next steps that lead to productive solutions and outcomes. For example, "How can you validate your problem statement?" or "Who might you ask for input on your solution set?" are certainly leading questions, but the coachee still owns the answer and the action. We call these *Guiding Questions*.

The second type are *Reflection Questions*. When designed properly and asked at the right time in the right way, these questions are almost impossible to answer right away. They often should invoke some silence, because the very question forces the individual to think. Some of these questions are just about the right timing. My first and probably most influential mentor was Dan Meckley. When I would visit him and provide an update on my life or career, he could sense when I was telling him a story that I was still living the story and not learning from the story, so he would ask, "What did you learn from that?" I usually did not want to face that question quite yet, but I often needed it, and as my mentor, he provided the reflection moment.

If you compare this to the PDSA coaching cycle that is explained in the previous chapter, you might use more of the Guiding Questions during the Plan and even Do phases of work, and the Reflection Questions during the Study phase of the work. The idea is to set yourself up for learning using the Guiding Questions and deepen the learning with the Reflection Questions. Some might think it is Guiding during problem solving and Reflecting after, but I find that if you wait until the end of problem solving to try to extract your lessons, then it is too late because you are too far removed from the learning moment.

From here, I will simply share examples of each type of question through generic phases of problem solving. As noted in chapter 2 about problem-solving tools, these phases can probably map into any tool or template you are using. Do not use my questions as your checklist but as a jumping-off point. When you pull a checklist "off the shelf," you are just going through the motions and cannot master coaching. Ultimately, you have to *earn* the right set of questions for yourself as a coach through your own experimentation and learning. Refer to the sections on behaviors and capabilities for more ideas on what questions will work for you or work for your coachees.

Getting Started (or Pre-Problem Solving)

Problem solving so often starts with problem statements, but this assumes at least two key things. First, that you decided to pick up the proverbial pen and get started. Second, that you were the right person to do so. These are big assumptions, and if you wait until you get past all that to start coaching someone—or a team—on problem solving, then you will never help build a capable ecosystem for problem solving. Effective coaches, particularly when embedded with their coachee in some form, begin before they get to the tool or task of problem solving.

Guiding Questions for Getting Started

- What information tells you what problems you currently have?
- How many problems can you identify right now?
- How might you sort those problems?
- Which problems do we already know the answer to?
- Which problems have you seen before?
- Which problems indicate a more systemic problem?

- Which problems do you own?

- Which problems will the true owner never see unless you take action?

- Which problems can be solved on your own?

- Which problems need cross-functional collaboration?

Reflection Questions for Getting Started

- Do you have the right sources of information to know your problem landscape?

- Do the most important problems find you, or do you have to look for them?

- What problems are going unidentified?

- What is your role in shaping the problem landscape?

- What is your role in sorting the problem landscape?

- Can every person identify which problems they own when they see them?

Problem Statements

Problem statements help frame and guide your problem-solving efforts. It is generally an area that is underinvested, which is why we dedicated an entire chapter to it (chapter 4). More time, collaboration, and even study are required to make the problem statements as effective as possible to guide future work. On the other hand, trying to be "right" can lead to wasted effort, because we should remain open to modifying our problem statements as we learn more through the steps that follow.

Guiding Questions for Problem Statements

- Do you have a standard? Was it followed? And did the standard still yield an unacceptable outcome?

- Do you have a clear metric or KPI (Key Performance Indicator) that shows an abnormal condition?

- Who first identified the problem? When did they identify it?

- Who is most impacted by the problem?

- Who needs to agree with the problem statement for the outcome to be successful?

- Who could you talk to who might have a different perspective on the problem?

- How could you test whether your problem statement is correct?

- How will you be able to test whether you have solved the problem when complete?

- Who do you need to be aligned with on the final problem statement?

- When do you need to go back and review whether the problem statement is still valid?

Reflection Questions for Problem Statements

- Are you always able to distinguish between normal and abnormal conditions?

- Are you able to capture problem statements objectively without implying cause or solution?

- How far do you take crafting a problem statement before you engage others?

- Are you always clear when a standard needs to be created, when an existing standard needs to be followed, and when an existing standard needs to be improved?

- How often does your first problem statement need to be modified as you head down the rest of the problem-solving steps?

- Are your problem statements more often too broad or too narrow?

Current Reality

The current reality is sometimes called root cause, but this is often limited for inherently complex problems where the gap is not a discrete defect and there is no single root cause. What you are really trying to determine is why the problem exists. You are trying to understand cause and effect, which was covered in chapter 5. You need to study the current state, and so the right coaching guide is to put someone on a learning path. They must close the knowledge gap before they close the problem statement gap.

Guiding Questions for Current Reality

Quite often, the first two questions may be all you need in this list:

- What do you not know or understand about your problem?

- What is the best way, or method, to learn?

- Is there a single root cause of a defect or error?

- Are there many contributors to the undesired outcome?

- Is the problem multidimensional?

- Do you need to break the problem into pieces or parts to understand why it exists?

Reflection Questions for Current Reality

- Are you more focused on what you already know or what you do not know?

- Do you have a favorite tool to understand current reality, and is that always helpful?

- How often do you learn more when you are closest to the point of activity of the problem?

- What has been more important, getting the right answer or getting the group involved in learning together?

- What happens when you select the wrong tool or method to study current reality?

- How important has this phase of work been to making the rest of problem solving much easier?

Target State

As I mentioned in the chapter on Ideal State (chapter 10), I have always found the target state one of the hardest phases of problem solving to coach, partly because it is less about methodology and more about mindset or behavior. What's key is that we are not talking as much about results (such as zero defects) but what good *looks* like. Focus more on the system or process, or the *how*. If there is a process map for the current reality, for example, then your target state would probably be a process map as well.

Guiding Questions for the Target State

- If you had no constraints, what would good look like?

- If [insert a great/respected company's or individual's name] ran this process, what would it look like? (For example, what would renewing your driver's license look like if it were run by Disney?)

- When you need this process to go fast by expediting, how fast can it go? Why can't it go that fast all the time?

- How many different ideas have you considered?

- What would the process look like if we focused only on the most important variable?

- How might we test our best idea?

- How might we test our crazy ideas?

Reflection Questions for the Target State

- When does the target state begin to take shape?

- How detailed does your target state need to be in order to be helpful?

- How has having a target state enabled you to move past obvious first solutions?

- What have been the most important capabilities to help create the target state?

- How do we separate our doubts, fears, and restrictions while creating our target state?

Action Plan

Actions plans should be, and quite frankly are, simpler to coach than the rest of the steps. However, if it goes wrong, everything you have done up to this point will be wasted, including the learning, because the learning is most effective when followed through to completion. A coach helps the individual see it through to the end.

Guiding Questions for the Action Plan

- Who will do what by when?

- What stands in the way of successfully completing the action plan?

- What help is needed to complete the action plan?

- What risks do you face in your action plan?

- Do you have the simplest action plan possible, allowing you to test?

- Do you have full alignment of everyone involved in taking action?
- What will happen if something goes wrong?

Reflection Questions for the Action Plan

- Are you still open to learning when you are focused on the action plan?
- Are you committed to your solution, or do you still consider this an experiment?
- Do new problems popping up get in the way of finishing solving this one?
- How important is alignment to completing the action plan?
- Do you prioritize what to finish or what to start?
- Do you wait for a polished action plan or use just enough to test?

Verification

Whether this is PDSA, experimentation, or testing (again, we're not prescriptive on problem-solving tools and templates here), you need to know the solution works. Because this is a learning phase, many of the guiding questions will sound like reflection questions. Here, the difference is what you are learning from the test, whereas reflection will be more about learning how to learn, which we covered in the Test to Learn chapter.

Guiding Questions for Verification

- Do you have a clear hypothesis of what result you will get when you make a change?

- Do you have a plan to observe the test?

- How will you collect any needed data?

- How will you ensure your test is valid?

- Did you get the result you were expecting? Why or why not?

Reflection Questions for Verification

- When is the best time to start to think about how you will test your proposed solution?

- What is more natural, testing a quick and dirty solution or implementing a "final" solution?

- What is more effective, testing or implementing?

- What is hard about making sure the test is relevant?

- How can you make your tests faster, cheaper, or easier?

As you use these questions, there are a few more things to consider. First, if the questions are not adding clarity to the phase of problem solving in which you are currently working, you may need to go back a step. For example, if the Current Reality questions are not leading you anywhere and you are stalled, maybe you do not have an effective problem statement and need to return to that part of the process.

As mentioned throughout the book, problem solving is about methodology but also about behavior and capability. Those dimensions are far harder to coach, and so most coaches tend to be overly focused on coaching methodology and tools. You must be able to pull the coachee into these other domains. Otherwise, problem solving will never be an embedded capability or culture, and coachees will apply only what they learned, which is primarily tools and templates.

Finally, do not ignore the value of using these questions for yourself. You can actually coach yourself, especially if you can cleanly separate doing and reflecting. You can create a set of questions for each step and grade yourself—or sit down and reflect. If you have a lot of problem-solving cycles, go deeper on different questions for different cycles. Develop small changes to your own standards for how you do problem solving. We all need a coach, but you can be your own coach when that is your only option.

19

Building Coaches

If you want to coach problem solving, then you need to build coaches. Far too few lean transformation road maps involve an explicit plan for doing so. They focus on training and try to train up a critical mass of their organization on problem solving. But what happens when someone finishes their training? They try to apply what they learned, they struggle, they may fail, and finally, they give up. Why? Because, especially in the early stages of our individual learning, we need coaches who help us close the gap between knowledge and capability, between understanding something and being able to use it. I have advised several companies to pump the brakes, slow down their training, and focus more on building coaching capacity, because otherwise, people would have become frustrated.

What is the target condition for an organization with coaches? Every employee should be no more than one degree removed from a coach. In other words, every employee should be able to access a coach where and when they need it. That means coaches must be plentiful, available, and connected. If an employee on the evening shift of a multishift operation has a problem they are engaged in solving, then what happens if all the coaches are on the day shift? Most likely, they never get the coaching they need because neither the problem nor the learning can wait.

Evaluate your coaching capacity by observing, or even surveying, with this question: Do you have access to a problem-solving coach where and when you need it? I do not recommend putting a lot of energy into trying to calculate a number, because it is often a moving target. As the learning increases, so does the demand for coaches, but then as the capability grows in the critical mass of the organization, the demand will drop, at least until you raise expectations again or the conditions get more complex for other reasons (a merger, a strategic pivot, or an economic crisis, as examples).

The Manager as Coach

There is one guaranteed way to ensure every employee is no more than one degree removed from a coach: make coaching the priority for every manager. One-on-one meetings become coaching sessions. Staff meetings can become shared-learning coaching sessions. The strongest lean organizations I have observed make this one of the core elements of their infrastructure.

Several supporting factors must also change to enable this goal. First, as discussed in other chapters, managers must make choices situation by situation about when they are a manager first and when they are a coach first. This is a trade-off between short-term performance and long-term capability for future performance. If the incentive system, both formal and cultural, is more focused on short-term performance than building long-term capability, then the manager-as-coach scheme will fail. As one former Toyota manager told me, "I cannot get promoted until my employees are capable of doing my job. My number-one priority is developing my team." The best signal you can send is in promotions, as this manager indicated. Not only will it be clear who "gets ahead" in the organization, but those managers, once promoted, will place value on this for their decisions.

Second, you need to build mechanisms and processes that enable this relationship. For example, look at your employee evaluation system. Is coaching built in or is its primary purpose to document and reward outcome-based performance? It can do both, but you can build the backbone of your system primarily for only one or the other.

Third, you need to think about how many team members a manager can coach without diluting and sacrificing quality. Organizations that are really focused on coaching often have a smaller span of control for each manager, but because they gain more from those employees as a result of the coaching, the payout is still positive. However, do not put the extra managers in place before you've built the capability.

Otherwise, you will have more managers committed to the old expectations and who build up greater resistance to becoming coaches. Instead, start shifting managers into being capable coaches, and they will gradually force the right ratio because they start to shape their environment to be optimal for coaching. I know one executive who makes an effort to keep their calendar very clear and open so they are available to their team for coaching or other needs. This is the kind of ownership of their coaching that managers should aspire to.

Here is the hard part: building that capability and culture, with that many managers, is difficult and takes time. It is a long-term decision to pursue this route. Not only do you face a real risk of managers diminishing what was working in order to shift to coaching, but they may not be good at it. They must learn, through practice, on their way to success. This means failures along the way. You must be accepting of those failures and perhaps supplement the organization with other crutches to prop it up during the transition.

I cannot think of many investments with a higher and more sustainable long-term payout than building an organization where every manager is a coach. However, I also cannot think of many investments that require more effort, persistence, and patience.

Who Else?

Beyond using every manager as a coach, there are basically two options left: full-time coaches or part-time coaches who make it part of their job either formally or informally.

Part-time coaches can be a formal expectation. It can be built into a job description or a role. This is often done with senior individual contributors or roles where the required skill set is already complementary to being a good problem-solving coach. This could include a Quality function where they probably already do a lot of problem solving or certain roles in HR that already do a lot of coaching.

The informal part-time coaches are often even more effective because most of these individuals coach because either they are truly passionate about coaching others in problem solving or they are so good they have a lot of demand for their help—or both. Many of these individuals cannot be full-time coaches because they are in roles they cannot be pulled them away from. They are too valuable as problem solvers in their domain. Some just help anyone who knocks on their door, and others set up formal "office hours" and advertise they are available to help. Most of the time, they are in such demand that I end up advising them to constrain their coaching and be more strategic in who they coach, but their momentum makes them help everyone they interact with to solve problems.

Full-time roles can be effective, as well, as these people are essentially required to make themselves available, or even strategically engage, where the coaching can be most effective. Most of the time, this is a role taken on by members of a "lean team," whether centralized or distributed. These resources can be embedded within teams, provide an access point where people can seek coaching, or establish formal coaching relationships with expectations for results.

Structures to Build Coaches

Building coaches takes more than encouragement and expectations. It requires building a system. The first, and perhaps most important, requirement is to have some standards for how to coach problem solving. This requirement goes beyond just having standards for how to solve problems. These standards might involve how to establish the role of a coach, all the way through following up. Imagine if in your organization, tomorrow, you just declared: "Everyone start coaching." The result would be chaos. You might move the organization but in a thousand different directions. Standards for coaching help you build consistency, provide a multiplier effect as one coach builds on another, and avoid confusion and frustration on the part of the coachees. Whether you put a rigorous control and enforcement mechanism in place for those coaching standards is a choice dependent on your culture, structure, and risk.

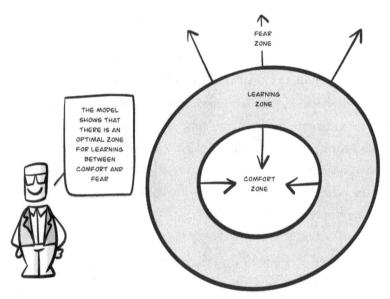

You also need to create space for individuals to learn how to coach. You might be familiar with this model of eliminating both comfort and fear from chapter 2 in *The Hitchhiker's Guide to Lean*. In short, the model shows there is an optimal zone for learning between comfort and fear. Comfort is where people spend most of their time, operating with conditions they are already familiar with. When you get too far outside your comfort zone, fear can set in. Both fear and comfort can be barriers to learning, and so to maximize learning, we want to shrink the comfort zone and push out the fear boundary.

Most coaches struggle to even get going with practice because of the fear of failure, either in the relationship or in the process. To be fair, there is a lot at stake. We must create safe opportunities to coach, such as with peers where they can practice and learn from each other. We could even establish peer forums to discuss how coaching will provide a safe mechanism that allows coaches to wade into the pool and learn how to coach.

Eliminating comfort is just as important. When potential coaches can continue to get stuff done using old and comfortable mechanisms, why would they jump into coaching? By shrinking, or eliminating, the comfort zone, you can deliberately push people into coaching. No one will feel comfortable at the beginning, so the idea that some-one can train and study enough to be "ready" is a fallacy. A potential coach must learn by doing. The simplest mechanism to eliminate the comfort zone is to make coaching an expectation. It might be the equivalent to learning to swim by being thrown into the water, but (a) that method works, and (b) if you have done all the other things, there is very little downside.

Coaches of Coaches

The most deliberate method to build coaching of problem solving is to have people coach the coaches. Both problem solving and coaching of problem solving are best learned by doing. Hence, the most direct way to help develop your coaching capability is to have "master coaches."

While coaches of problem solving must be highly competent at problem solving and competent in coaching, these master coaches do not necessarily need any deeper skills in problem solving, but they must have mastered coaching. There are two primary reasons for this. First is that coaching is the harder skill to cultivate in someone because it is more personal and varied. Second, the coach can improve their problem-solving skills while being a coach, as noted earlier. If you get the coach practicing coaching effectively, their problem-solving skills will naturally be honed along the way.

Coaches of coaches, if not full-time, should be easily identifiable and use standard practices and principles. Fellow coaches should be able to share experiences of being coached by a master coach. It's likely that most of your master coaches will emerge naturally because they simply value coaching so greatly as a way to affect people and performance that they will invest heavily in their own learning and practice. The more value the organization places on coaching, the easier it is for master coaches to emerge. If you do not recognize this as a valued capability, especially compared to more traditional skill sets that lead to career advancement, then finding and highlighting these coaches will be more difficult. These master coaches will also be the ones who develop, or at least should control, the standards for problem-solving coaching.

Coaching problem solving, as perhaps implied by how much time in the book we are focusing on the topic, is the greatest leverage point you have to drive effective problem solving. Build coaches, standards, and systems that support them in a purposeful way. This investment will surely pay off.

SECTION 5

The Role of the Leader

We have already covered perhaps the most important role of a leader, which is the opportunity to coach. It was crucial enough to devote the entire previous section to it. However, there is much more to the role of the leader in a problem-solving environment.

"Leader" can mean different things in different contexts. For our purposes, we are primarily talking about someone who manages direct reports, whether as a frontline manager or the CEO or anything in between. This is not the definition I usually use, because just as individual contributors can be leaders, people with direct reports are not always leading. However, if you are doing what we describe in this section, you are indeed a leader.

We start by describing the responsibility of the leader to be the system architect who helps make problem solving possible in chapter 20. In chapter 21, the leader must create experiences to build the culture we described throughout section 3. In chapter 22, we examine how a leader can and should get involved in their team's problems and help shape their efforts, which will be distinguished from the problems they own themselves in chapter 23.

20

The Leader as System Architect

Too often, managers at all levels operate the same way during the lean journey as they did before, just with some lean lingo thrown in for good measure. They might ask someone to do an A3 and feel they are doing their part for the journey. But a manager has responsibilities in the journey that go beyond using the words and supporting the journey with resources. For starters, they must be an architect of the system of work that drives effective problem solving.

What does that mean to be the *system architect*? It means that you take responsibility and ownership of the systems of work that expose problems, capture them, manage them, put resources to them, and ultimately, solve them. Sending people to problem-solving training might fall into that category, but that is the easy step and far from sufficient to build an effective problem-solving organization.

Some of the key elements we will explore could, or should, be organizational standards. But someone needs to set these standards, and senior management should be highly engaged in this process. How much they should be standardized across an organization is worthy of some debate and depends on the organization, the existing culture, the change strategy, and the level of maturity. However, even if you adopt a strong bias toward organizational standardization, there is still much work to be done by each director or manager for their own team's work. Standards for this work are rarely much more than guidelines, perhaps with a few IT tools thrown in. The reason for this is that all problem solving is contextual, and you must shape your systems for the nature and content of your work.

The Landscape of Problems

We begin with what I like to call the *landscape of problems*. There are many sources of problems and many sources of finding those problems. Yet most teams end up deciding what problem to engage with next rather randomly, without respect to the entire landscape. Consider these many sources:

- You probably have key metrics, or Key Performance Indicators, that you monitor. When properly designed, they should have a clear definition of when things are normal and when they are abnormal. When a key metric hits an abnormal level, problem solving could be initiated.

- You may have standard work that helps you consistently perform your team's tasks. However, sometimes there is a problem and the standard cannot be followed or ceases to work as designed. This condition could drive problem solving.

- You do audits of the work, ranging from a simple 5S audit[19] to a complex customer process audit. These audits generally produce findings, each of which can be defined as a problem.

---

19   5S is a workplace organization method popular in lean manufacturing. The 5S elements are: Sort (Seiri), Set in Order (Seiton), Shine (Seiso), Standardize (Seiketsu), and Sustain (Shitsuke).

- You develop a culture of identifying waste using the lens of the seven wastes and perform waste walks of the process. Each waste occurrence found is a problem that could be solved.

- You fail to meet a deliverable to a customer, internal or external. You are asked what will be done about it, which means you have a problem that needs to be solved and reported back to that customer.

- Your team is frustrated with something, and it is a persistent topic of conversation and drag on the team. They would like the problem fixed.

And there are more sources of problems. Here is the challenge: if each source of potential problems is managed and reacted to independently, you have no strategy for what problems you really should be solving. The simplest way to manage your landscape of problems strategically is to have a single list of problems regardless of where the problem is found, but a single list does not have to be your solution.

As a leader, you must have an awareness of all the sources of problem identification and a system of work for examining and engaging with them in a balanced and purposeful way. You must have a systematic approach to managing your problem landscape. Otherwise, your team will react to each next problem that pops up in their inbox, which gives you extraordinarily little control of managing your improvement path.

The Andon, or Help Chain

A core element of your system is how you connect help to any problem as it occurs. *Andon* (which I briefly referred to in chapter 10) is a Japanese word meaning "lantern," which relates to our situation as a signal light to indicate that there is a problem. If you prefer words that are more descriptive for your use, I like to call this the *help chain* because it is what connects help to the problem occurrence. While not every problem in your problem landscape will receive systematic problem solving, every problem should receive attention.

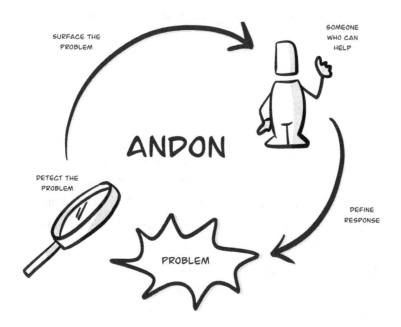

To do this, you must define all five elements that are context-specific to the environment in which you work. First, you must define those problems that should be escalated and those that should not. For example, if your process takes five to six days, is that a problem or just natural variation of your work? More importantly, if *I* think you have a problem at four days and *you* don't think it is a problem until you reach seven days, then in between those two markers, we are going to have plenty of frustrating tension. We should have the same definition of what is a problem.

Next, you need a way to notice the problem. This is one of the reasons that, in a lean environment, we strive to make the work as visual as possible so it is easier to detect the problem. Again, this is extremely specific to the nature of the work and must be solved at a local level.

Third, you need a method to escalate the problem. What is the one, and ideally only one, way to surface that problem? The reason for the term *andon* is that the original creation of this approach was in a manufacturing environment at Toyota where a light would turn on and music would play. But a pilot declaring "Mayday" is a code word that accomplishes the same task, as is an error message popping up on your computer. There are many ways to create a signal, but it should be simple, timely, and very clear. These three elements make up the *request* for help.

The next two elements make up the *response* to that request. We must determine who is the right person to respond. This is often assumed to be the immediate manager, but this is the case only if they are able to provide the necessary help. Make sure the right resource is connected, either to coach or to solve. And finally, how do they respond, and just as importantly, when do they respond? This should be standardized so the other end of that help chain is not wondering whether, when, and in what form that help is going to arrive.

Managing and Prioritizing the Problems

Whether you are managing ten problems or a hundred, you need some method to ensure they are captured and being worked on. If they exist somewhere in an email thread from five days ago or scribbled in the margin of someone's notebook, that is not a very reliable or transparent system. You may determine you want a single team list that is easy for everyone to monitor, but again, the details should fit your needs and your team's work environment.

There are a couple of elements that are important to include. Ownership of the problem should be clear. A team cannot own a problem, because when it stalls, who do I look to for an explanation? Even if the person who owns it is doing only a small portion of the work, there has to be a person clearly accountable for pushing the problem forward.

Progress made is also important to understand. It is easy for problems to stall, but they must be pushed through whatever barriers were holding them back. All of this should be transparent. Knowing what is being worked on, and what is not, is not only useful inside the team, but it is also useful to those higher up the organizational chart and out to your internal customers and suppliers.

Within that system, prioritization is also important. If your team is very proficient at both solving problems and keeping them small, then first in, first out is a great and simple system. You manage the inbound on the problem landscape, and then once you start them, you push through to the end without interruption.

However, if your problems are too large or your capacity to solve them is too small, problems tend to linger. Then you need to dynamically prioritize the set of problems being worked on. I suggest focusing on prioritizing what to finish rather than what to start. It is easy to start new problems, but what needs to get finished? Getting finished means you are able to realize the performance benefits but also the learning and the sense of accomplishment. The latter two are the fuel that allows you to get the next problem done as well. Focus on getting problems finished.

Build Capacity and Capability

No matter how well-developed your system for managing problems, it will perform only as well as your team's capacity and capability to solve problems. As a leader, it is your responsibility to build both.

Capability is relatively straightforward. Who is trained? Who is practicing? Who is at what level of competence? The most important aspect that you must determine is where everyone will go for coaching help. Coaching is the main lifeblood of problem-solving capability, as we made clear in the previous section of the book. Everyone in your organization should be, ideally, one step removed from a coach. Maybe you, as the leader, are going to act as the coach. Are you prepared for that? Will you make yourself available on their terms and not your terms? It is usually not the willingness to coach but the willingness to design your own work around being available to be a coach that is the bigger challenge.

Maybe the coach is someone within your team. They will have the same challenge. When you say, "Lisa will be our coach," then through whatever means you manage your team's workload, that must be taken into account. Coaching cannot stop just because Lisa has a busy month ahead.

Capacity is a bit trickier. Over time, as we solve more problems, our work becomes more stable, and we end up with greater capacity. But today, we still must "carve out" or "make" time for problem solving. In part, this is the culture of initiative that was described in chapter 13. This is much easier to do at the team or organizational level than at the individual level.

Building capacity begins with properly valuing time spent in problem solving relative to other work. The work never all gets done before everyone goes home at the end of the day. Therefore, some stuff gets done and other work does not. How do you decide? Based on what you value! If you value polishing PowerPoint and attending every meeting you are invited to more than you value problem solving, then that is the work that will get done and problem solving will have to wait. As the leader, you have to first decide, and then communicate, how much problem solving is valued.

Then you must develop a system that ensures the work gets done. If you look at your employees' calendars and they have five review meeting notices from you but nothing carved out for problem solving, it sends a pretty clear signal of what is important. The easiest way to signal the importance is to commit the team's time. This could be done by blocking off an hour a day, or an afternoon, or some form of clear capacity commitment. It is your system of work and your system of priorities. How will your decisions signal what you value? How will you design your team's system to drive the priority?

We all work as part of a system. As a leader, you are responsible for this system of work getting the right things done. Your role is to be an architect and design your system with purpose.

21

Building Culture

In section 3 of the book, we described six behaviors that define an effective problem-solving culture. Cultures may be built accidentally, but then you will not get the culture you want. Building the culture requires deliberate action on the part of a leader to generate experiences for people.

Our beliefs and principles are shaped by experiences. Those beliefs and principles, in turn, drive our behaviors. The questions are: What experiences are shaping your team's thinking, and are they shaping the thinking in the desired direction? Most managers underestimate the impact of their words and actions and how they affect the behaviors of the team or organization. It's made more complicated when, while you are creating deliberate experiences, other leaders unintentionally create conflicting experiences and your job becomes much harder. The fact that it is hard is why most managers don't even bother being deliberate about shaping their culture. However, this is too important to not make central to your role as a leader. If you get the culture right, as hard as that can be, then everything else becomes easier. If you had an organizational culture that lived the behaviors in section 3 every single day and at every level of the organization, you would hardly need anything else in this book. Here are a few areas where leaders can create deliberate experiences that help shape an effective problem-solving culture.

Design the System

This was already covered in the last chapter, but we will start here because of the system's impact on the culture. When you choose to spend your time as a leader working on the system of work and designing aspects of the process to help the team manage their problems, that will clearly indicate that you consider how you solve problems to be important.

How you design the system also helps shape the culture. For example, if you do block off time for everyone to work on problems, you can use that time to check in with people working on their problems. First, you ensure the accountability that tells people this was not just a suggestion. Second, you get to ask what help is needed, whether it is removing a barrier or providing some coaching. This creates a deliberate spot on your calendar to actually be a visible leader in the problem-solving arena, and that will affect how people see problem solving.

Role-Model the Behaviors

If you do everything else in this chapter right but fail to role-model the behaviors desired yourself, then you will negate most of your efforts. This goes only so far to create the culture, but it certainly can destroy it.

An old story about Mahatma Gandhi illustrates this point. I do not know whether the story is true or folklore, but it certainly demonstrates the character that the man embodied. He would frequently hold court, meeting his many followers. One mother was very frustrated with her son because he was eating too much sugar and she could not get him to stop no matter what she tried. As she had run out of ideas, she took the boy to visit Gandhi, walking many miles and waiting in line for hours. When she finally got to see Gandhi, she explained her trouble. Gandhi listened, looked at the boy, and told them to come back in two weeks.

Two weeks passed, and she returned with her son, walking the same many miles and waiting in line for hours. Gandhi put his hand on the boy, looked him in the eye, and told him to stop eating sugar and that it was bad for his health. A bit frustrated, the mother asked why he could not have done that two weeks ago. He explained that two weeks ago, he was eating too much sugar, and he needed to stop that habit before he could ask the boy to stop. The message behind this is that the *credibility* of both your words and actions depend on what you personally demonstrate.

The mistake many leaders make, however, is they do not understand that the demonstration must be visible. If no one sees you do it, you are not a role model. They will tell me they are a lean thinker and a thoughtful problem solver and that lean thinking is going on in their brain all the time. However, if I ask their team, they think the leader has not even engaged with deliberate problem solving. One of two things is possible. Either the leader is kidding themselves that they are thinking lean all the time or they are thinking lean but no one believes it because they cannot see it. As it applies to creating the right problem-solving culture, both reasons are failures.

This means you must look for and sometimes even create opportunities to demonstrate the desired behaviors. This might feel like bravado or showing off. It will probably be uncomfortable. You must make sure you are not constructing false playacting situations; they must still be genuine demonstrations. Fundamentally, role-modeling the behaviors is the minimum threshold for creating the desired culture.

Establish and Reinforce Clear Expectations

It is important to set the tone that participating is not optional. You may have some things you will encourage more, but you must set some minimum expectations that you not only practice yourself but also use to hold others accountable. It is often more effective if the expectations are narrowly defined so the pattern of reinforcement is stronger. But what you select to hold people accountable for provides a foundation on which to build the rest of the culture. For example, unrelated to problem solving, if you want to build a culture of cleanliness and tidiness, you might focus on "If you see trash, pick it up," and make sure you very visibly demonstrate that behavior wherever possible. You do not need to drive the full comprehensive culture you want all at once, but start with a foundational behavior that can naturally lead to others.

I coached one leader in problem solving who became obsessed (in a good way) with getting people to start with a problem statement. In just about every meeting, and certainly with every proposal or idea someone brought him, his response was, "What problem are you trying to solve?" This became so well-known throughout his very large organization that even people who didn't work with the leader knew this was the expectation. Do not try to fix something unless you are clear about the problem statement. This behavior isn't representative of the entire problem-solving culture desired, but it was a great start, and once people had a problem statement, it made them more curious about learning the rest of the problem-solving behaviors and skills.

In another organization, they had developed a system around problem solving that involved boards and huddles at every level of the organization. The expected behavior was that problems were captured on these boards. Everyone had permission to add a problem to each other's board as a method of "request," including up to your boss's board. If you put a problem on someone else's board, a response was required, even if that response was that they did not think they should own that problem or they wanted to push it back down to your team. The senior leader of this organization frequently had the opportunity to reinforce the behavior of using the system. Someone would stop him in the hallway, send him an email, or casually mention something before a meeting started about a problem that they have observed. Before they got to finish, his response was, "Is the problem on the board?" If the answer was no, he cut them off and did not let them talk about the problem. There was a standard, and he held people accountable for following that standard. This ensured there were not two sets of problems, the set that is on the boards and the set we do not write down but talk about in hallways.

As a leader, your job is to practice *relentless patience*. This is a term I like to use about the cultural journey. You demonstrate *patience* for people to master all the capabilities required and the behaviors that support them. Mastering problem solving is a lifelong journey, and we should not expect anyone to master it just because they attended a training class on using the tools. However, at the same time, leaders must demonstrate impatience (that's the *relentless* part) about being on the journey. Do not let people sit on the sidelines and wait you out. Insist they make an effort, because this is how they learn. Choose a behavior or two that you will be relentless about, such as the examples above, so you start laying the foundation of a problem-solving culture.

Support Your Team

Many leaders do not have a clear picture of what support looks like in a problem-solving environment. They treat support as a binary role, either heavily involved or hands-off. But there is a proper role for leaders to play that combines engagement with empowerment.

If you care a great deal about the outcome and have a clear vision for where the solution space must go, then do not delegate the problem ownership. Own it yourself. I will find myself coaching a leader who is, in turn, trying to coach their team on a problem, but the team is not heading where the leader wants them to go. Well then, why did you delegate it? Own it, because your effort to delegate and empower sets false expectations and sets everyone up for failure.

The leader has the biggest impact on the front end of problem solving. You can have a lot to say about prioritizing the problem and the problem statement itself. Ensure people are working on a problem that you agree is worth solving. You should also have a lot to say about who is involved. Whether it is insisting on or even assigning a coach, or requiring the problem being solved is worked on collaboratively with an internal partner, these early decisions set the tone for the path that will be followed. The last part that can be established up front are the boundary conditions, making sure the team stays in their lane, and the conditions of satisfaction.

Setting the conditions of satisfaction is quite difficult for leaders to learn. It requires their own reflection and learning about what they are looking for in the solution space. You must pull from some of the intuition you have developed through practice, coaching, and reflection. Think of all the reasons you have balked when teams have presented solutions in the past; there is probably some clarity around what you are looking for before you will accept a solution. It might be that you require the solution be tested, that they have validated it with the customer, or that they selected a fast, simple solution over the expensive, elegant solution. It can be quite unfair to the team if you empower them to solve the problem only to show them where the finish line is when they fail to cross it. This is an easy way to crush the energy and commitment to problem solving in your organization.

Throughout problem solving, you need to be available and engaged but not interfere. If someone is closest to the problem, has the skills, and is digging deeper into current reality than you are, then you must trust in the person and the process. However, you should be available for two primary needs. The first is to provide resources or remove barriers. Those barriers could be that they cannot get participation from a key resource or they cannot get access to data or to the environment in which they are solving the problem. The second need is to provide clarity around the boundary conditions and conditions of satisfaction, as above. While we seek to make this clear in the beginning, we want to make sure the team, before they stall or spin even a little, feels comfortable asking for clarity.

For example, I was working with a team that was working on a process layout problem, trying to improve lead time and quality for a particular process. There were numerous solutions they were considering, but they had stalled because there was clearly one best solution. However, that solution was determined as a nonstarter because it would violate what they perceived as a boundary condition of what they could and could not move. As the leader happened to be walking by, I pulled him in so they could ask for clarification. His response: "Yes, if that's the best solution, go ahead and move whatever needs to move." Immediately, the team went from stalled low-energy and frustration to high-energy and committed action.

Perhaps the most important aspect of supporting your team is not second-guessing their work. Two housemates are discussing what to have for dinner. The first friend asks the second what they would like to eat. The second replies, "I don't care. You decide." The first suggests pizza, and the response is, "No, I don't want pizza." Either the first housemate was empowered to make the decision or they were not. As a leader, it is important not to send mixed signals. Otherwise, people will naturally slide all their problem-solving efforts toward the solutions they think you want to see rather than bringing their analysis and creativity to the problem. This will not only fail to get the best ideas on the table, but problem solving itself will be a wasteful charade.

This does not mean you do not engage at the end. Ask questions. Understand the thinking behind the solutions. If you are wondering why they did not look at a particular solution, then it is likely that at the beginning you should have communicated: "Make sure you at least look at this solution as an option."

Overall, how you engage, empower, and support the team throughout the problem-solving endeavor influences the effectiveness of it a lot. If you are not getting the behaviors you want, then start by looking in the mirror. It is likely you have had a strong hand in creating the culture you currently observe. Cultures are created, in part, by leaders. You get either an accidental culture you did not intend or a deliberate culture you helped shape.

22

Shaping Problem Solving

As you act as a leader by designing the architecture of your problem-solving system and building your problem-solving culture, you also have the role of being engaged in day-to-day problem solving. This goes beyond the problems you personally solve, which we will cover in the next chapter, and instead focuses on how you engage in and shape your team's problem-solving efforts.

Acting as a coach is perhaps the most powerful role you can practice to be engaged in your team's problem solving, and we have dedicated an entire section of this book to the practice of coaching. But beyond coaching, there are three important and specific roles you can play to be effectively engaged. They are: drawing the line between firefighting and problem solving, shaping the problem scope, and reducing the friction of problem solving across boundaries.

Call a Band-Aid a Band-Aid

A common mistake I see companies make in their problem-solving journey is they either think or pretend they are doing structured problem solving for everything and they consider firefighting, putting

Band-Aids on problems, or doing anything not worthy of being called "structured problem solving" to be a failure. It is not. If you are honest about your definition of a problem, if you attempted to get to the root cause of every abnormal condition you experienced, progress would grind to a halt. There is no way we can handle that kind of workload. Some problems just require a Band-Aid.

If your computer crashes, do you halt your progress until you find the root cause, or do you try a reboot and see if everything works out fine? If a single meeting starts late, do you try to remind everyone about the importance of being on time and see if the problem goes away? If someone does not understand an instruction, do you simply restate it in another way and see whether it is now clear? None of these were true problem-solving solutions. At no point did you define the problem statement or seek an understanding of the root cause. The problem was inherently small enough, and the experience suggesting a possible course of action sound enough, that you could proceed with a solution. If those problems persist and our experience and intuition-driven solutions prove ineffective, then we might decide to engage in structured problem solving for a more effective solution and outcome.

When organizations fail to acknowledge that this type of firefighting through basic troubleshooting and putting Band-Aids on issues is not only occurring but is necessary, they create a false expectation of where problem solving fits into the organization. That false expectation usually leads to many half-hearted efforts, such as completing the problem-solving templates after the solution has been decided. It can destroy the credibility of what defines good problem solving.

It is much cleaner to call a Band-Aid a Band-Aid, call firefighting what it is, and acknowledge openly that structured problem solving is not the only acceptable path forward. Once you do this, you allow a more honest and useful discussion about when to firefight and when to let problem solving emerge. Your job as a leader is to help make those decisions. More often than not, this is about when to push people toward structured problem solving when the firefighting efforts prove ineffective. However, it can also be about helping people recognize when the weight of the problem and the confidence of the instinctive answer means the investment of time and effort is better spent elsewhere.

Why isn't this topic in the chapter on designing the architecture of an effective system? Because not only is the line very difficult to define, it is a moving target that depends on your capacity, your strategy, your priorities, and even the relative problem-solving maturity of your team. Being active begins with being aware of both the set of issues being dealt with and how your team is making the determination.

Then engage on an active basis to help draw the line toward optimizing your team's effort and energy on problem solving.

Shaping the Problem Scope

The delegation or empowerment of problem solving downward into the organization does not mean being hands-off or passive. As I've already mentioned, if you care greatly about the outcome, then sometimes you should not delegate and instead just own the problem solving yourself.

There are other ways to be engaged and have an impact on where problem solving goes without disempowering people. Invest your time on the front end rather than the back end. On the back end, leaders second-guess or even dismiss solutions, rethink the work, or discredit the effort taken to achieve the conclusions. All of these reactions disempower the individual or team, who is left legitimately thinking, *Why don't you just tell us what solution you want?*

Instead, invest time on the front end helping shape the direction and boundary conditions of the problem-solving effort. In the book *The Primes*,[20] the author introduced the *Rule of Parity*. Simply stated: "People need approximately as much space to talk about the problem as they do the solution." You have a hand in slowing down the team and providing that space. If you do not invest time in the problem, then solutions have nothing to attach to and are born out of nothing or from half-thoughts and half-truths. A leader's job, and their influence, can greatly reduce the waste of human talent by ensuring there are thoughtful and aligned problem statements before too much work is conducted. If a leader masters only one capability from section 1, it should be the crafting of problem statements.

---

20   Chris McGoff, *The Primes: How Any Group Can Solve Any Problem* (Hoboken, New Jersey: Wiley, 2012), xxviii.

This effort adds discipline to problem solving, and that discipline ensures the team and the leader are never too far apart. David Campbell, the founder of Saks Fifth Avenue, said, "Discipline is remembering what you want."[21] Problem solving requires discipline. It is easy to jump through steps, find an easy path or shortcut, solve an entirely different problem, or end up with scope creep of the problem you are solving. But rather than rely on individual or team discipline to stay focused and true to the process, there is a trick.

Begin every discussion by returning to the problem statement. First, repeat it out loud. Remind everyone what the team is working on. Second, ask and verify whether it is still the right problem statement. This is one of those situations where you cannot just let the question hang for half a second and move on if there are no objections. You need to look people in the eye and see their reaction, even hesitation, about the question. Find the conflict or discomfort and draw it out into the open.

The first part provides the discipline. The problem statement establishes your vector, or direction, where you want to head. Any step or idea that does not help you advance your problem should be avoided or, at most, captured somewhere out of the way to be dealt with later. If the problem statement has the proper investment, it provides a means to continually align—or realign, if necessary—the team and maintains their focus and discipline.

By asking whether it is still the right problem statement, you help apply the discipline of learning and an open mind. You will often learn things throughout the problem-solving process that should shape or change your problem statement. In my experience, this is more than half of the time. The easiest path is to keep charging ahead with what

---

21   Chris McGoff, *The Primes: How Any Group Can Solve Any Problem* (Hoboken, New Jersey: Wiley, 2012), 7.

you have; after all, you have invested all this time already. But that is the sunk cost fallacy, and even if you have invested thousands of hours, if you are moving in the wrong direction, then the next hour invested is still wasted. Stopping to purposefully adjust your scope through your problem statement requires a discipline of its own, and this question helps maintain that discipline.

The boundary conditions of the problem-solving effort can be equally important, and the leader can either set them or ensure they are set in a thoughtful manner. There are both positive and negative boundary conditions. Positive boundary conditions are factors that must be part of the solution. For example, you might allow the team to develop any solution they want "as long as it's compatible with SAP." You are not going to rip out an enterprise software solution because one specific problem has a better solution for itself. Your positive boundary condition could be around time, such as, "It must be implemented by November." The team might have a better solution that can be implemented next March, but you would prefer (or require) a suboptimal solution by November, perhaps because of a customer or government requirement. These boundary conditions may not come into play until someone is evaluating potential solutions, but it still helps frame the work ahead of that step rather than to reacting to the potential solutions with your first articulation of what really matters.

Negative boundary conditions are things you must avoid and are just as dangerous to the effort if not defined early. For example, you might say, "You cannot ask the customer to change their process." It might be more effective to ask the customer for a change, but if the relationship is already on edge, then that might be a path you choose to avoid. The most common of these negative boundary conditions involves capital restrictions, either none at all or limits on what the team can spend to solve the problem (see the chapter on Creativity over Capital for more).

Building Bridges for Problem Solving

If you are like most organizations, some of your biggest, and certainly most challenging, problems span across organizational boundaries. Most of these problems require some level of collaboration, and certainly some alignment, before progress can be made. We would prefer that the organizational culture enables teams to cross over boundaries in seamless collaboration to solve such problems, which is why we dedicated a chapter to the behavior of collaboration. However, where culture does not provide that bridge, the leader's job is to build a bridge across these organizational spans to enable collaboration and alignment.

The following example shows how most efforts appear (described in more detail in chapter 12). Team A sees a problem that involves Team B. This could be anything as different as operations and accounting or as similar as two different shifts in the same unit. Team A begins solving the problem, doing all sorts of good and noble work, to finally come up with a solution. They then take the solution to Team B as a final proposal to be accepted or rejected. Then, when it is predictably rejected, either overtly or as a "pocket veto"[22] by not acting on the recommendation, the team approaches their leader looking for help to get Team B to comply.

There is a legitimate reason for this behavior. When Team A tries to proactively engage Team B at the beginning of the process, they are also met with resistance. This is when and where the leader must engage.

This engagement may not always go the way Team A wants. The leader's job is not to get the other team to comply but instead to engage. The type of engagement needed determines what kind of bridge the leader must build. First, true collaboration is most necessary when there is alignment on the priority of the problem and both the evidence needed and the potential solution is found on both sides of the relationship. The leader may need to negotiate, but there must be a shared interest in making this collaboration work effectively.

Another scenario is where there is alignment on the priority of the problem but the majority of evidence and/or leverage to solve the problem is found on only one side of the relationship. The role of the leader is to ensure the alignment is in place, and since collaboration

---

22   Pocket veto: an indirect veto of a legislative bill by the US president or a state governor by retaining the bill unsigned until it is too late for it to be dealt with during the legislative session. – *Oxford English Dictionary*, s.v. "pocket veto."

will necessarily be more fragmented, there is at least an agreement about how to proceed and stay connected.

The most difficult scenario is when there is not an alignment on priority but the evidence and/or leverage to solve the problem is on both sides of the relationship. In this situation, it is quite difficult to get collaboration because one of the parties has, by definition, more important things to do. The leader must sort out how important a priority this problem is to the broader organization. In my opinion, this relates directly to how much it involves the value experienced (or not experienced, as is the case of most problems) by the customer. If it is impacting the customer, then it should be moving up everyone's priority list. This might not change things and might actually expose that the other team is already working entirely on problems that impact the customer, and therefore changing their attention to "our problem" is a bad decision. In these cases, the leader must help the team reframe the problem to figure out what they can do without collaboration. Not every problem that benefits from collaboration will get collaboration. The leader must navigate these waters.

More broadly, the leader should ensure the team has the right amount of collaboration across their problem landscape. If there are too many problems that require slower-moving collaboration, the team's overall momentum and attitude may stall. Not enough collaboration, and they might not be working on high-leverage problems. This is a balancing act that the leader must take as their responsibility.

23

Solving Your Problems

The role of a manager in problem solving is different from that of an individual contributor. Whether you are a frontline manager of five people or a CEO covering thirty thousand people, your team has lots of problems. As the overall accountable person for that team, large or small, that means you have lots of problems too. Many of us can feel overwhelmed by all of these problems, burdened by the never-ending sheer volume of problems. Like the idiom of the straw that broke the camel's back or the last drop of water that made the cup run over, there can be a feeling that if one more problem were to surface, then either you, the team, or the organization might shatter.

The measure of a leader can often be determined, falsely, by how many straws they can carry without breaking. This is the wrong measure of success, yet in some organizations, this can be perceived as the pathway to promotion. Instead of simply carrying the straw, we must learn to strategically manage the straw, as when done right (at risk of overextending the metaphor), a team of camels pulling a cart of straw can manage much more than many individual camels carrying it on their backs. Are you the manager of a team dealing with problems or just another team member trying to help carry the load?

The Twenty-Five Problems Myth

If you are a manager with five direct reports, imagine each of your five direct reports has five problems on their plate (or straws on their back). Do you, as their manager, have twenty-five problems? The observable behavior of most managers and executives would suggest this is their belief. They want to know about those problems, their status, and their magnitude, and they often use this information to determine which of those problems they should get engaged with directly and bring their problem-solving muscle to bear to resolve the issue.

However, this is the myth. Seeing your team's problems as your own problems makes you little more than just a senior team member. You miss your leverage. You miss what is going on just below the surface of those visible problems with the system underneath. These twenty-five problems are the visible problems. They must be solved, or at least resolved, even if with a Band-Aid. However, if you worry only about their resolution, you are missing all the less-visible information that you, as the manager, must own and ultimately use to resolve different problems.

This means that as a manager, you do not have twenty-five problems but five newly found and articulated problems that are extracted from what is learned from the first twenty-five. To the manager who feels overwhelmed, this can appear counterintuitive because it now feels like you have thirty problems. However, it is your leverage of the five new problems that really moves you forward and takes you out of the chaos or burden of the twenty-five. That is because these are not five new problems—they're new only to you. They already existed within your team.

This does not mean you ignore those twenty-five problems, because they are all symptoms of your system and therefore carry useful insights to find the leverage for new systemic problem solving. By engaging in those twenty-five problems, either as a coach or an observer, you learn the ground truth about what is going on in your team or your organization that can lead to insight into what types of problems you should be solving. Those twenty-five problems are symptoms of either your system of work, your culture, or your capability.

In terms of capability, you may learn the team is poor at defining problems, at getting to root causes, or at collaborating through problem solving. If you dig past the surface-level information of the problems, you may see capability gaps that you take responsibility for solving as your own problem. If you close that capability gap, all of your team's problem solving will improve.

In terms of culture, you may notice patterns of behavior in the problems you observe. For example, you may observe that problems are captured only when they are for other people to resolve and therefore teams are not being honest and transparent about their own problems. Or perhaps you observe that people whip through their problem-solving templates without true curiosity to understand cause and effect and this leads to solutions that are at best Band-Aids.

In terms of the system of work, you may find patterns in the set of problems that indicate a broader systemic problem that you can take ownership to solve. For example, the teams might spend a lot of time resolving conflicts in prioritization, leading to an insight that your management system of prioritization is flawed, whether too ambiguous, too slow, or too conflicted. You may observe that there are multiple delays and errors between two different functions, each resolved piecemeal but leading to an insight into how these two functions systematically work together. Many of these insights either can be seen only at the pattern level because it requires piecing together many disconnected smaller pieces of evidence, or the system of work that is flawed is owned at the manager level and therefore the team cannot solve it.

What is most challenging in seeing past the twenty-five problems myth, or the twenty-five hundred problems myth, is that most of the information about the systemic problems that the leader must solve is still contained at the frontline level of work. For a frontline manager, this is a fairly direct level of observation, and therefore it is much easier for them to see their systematic issues. For an executive or CEO, the information that often comes to them through multiple levels of aggregation and abstraction does not always help them see the true pattern of the problems they must take owner-ship of. The ground truth of what individual contributors deal with in terms of problems, once aggravated and abstracted, is often lost. Hence, any insights it may provide can be clouded. Executives must combine the systems of information designed for them with enough direct observation of the actual work and problems that individ-uals deal with. Then the executives can gain insights about what is actually happening and what systemic problems they can own that generate high-leverage impact.

Taking on this new role is powerful but also can be scary. Those twenty-five, or twenty-five hundred, problems are still there, and you are still accountable for the results they threaten. However, that is now where your leverage is found. My former business partner and retired executive vice president of manufacturing at Chrysler, Denny Pawley, began the company's journey in this way in the 1990s. Every day, he had a sheet of paper on his desk that had the performance of each one of his thirty-six factories from around the world. Denny had an incredible technical problem-solving mind, and he could troubleshoot any bad news he found in that daily report. However, the fires would not stop, and he took a different approach.

He asked that this piece of paper not be on his desk anymore. He wasn't going to try to solve each day's fires but instead invest his time in solving the more systemic problems, such as the culture and capability of the organization. He was still accountable for those problems, and they needed to be solved. It takes a combina-tion of courage and conviction to stop fighting the fires and go to find higher-leverage problems to truly solve.

The Manager as Problem-Solving Capacity

In the spirit of lean being a methodology that helps to empower employees, this is often misinterpreted as an indication that managers should only empower problem solving and not be directly involved themselves. This is a mistake. Managers should be very active in problem solving, sometimes through empowerment, sometimes through coaching, and yes, also quite active in owning problems directly. This is not about disempowering employees, but when done correctly, supporting them.

I will define the engagement at three different levels. The first level can best be described as a clear division of labor between normal and abnormal work or sometimes standard and off-standard work. When the work of the team requires that they stay focused on execution, then the only way they can engage in problem solving is to either stop the work or assign it to someone else to solve it in parallel to the work continuing. For example, whether you are on a factory assembly line, in the middle of fighting an actual fire, or a programmer generating code for a customer, taking time to solve problems involves stopping the work at hand. This cannot always be done—or cannot be done without the cost of lost capacity.

In many of these cases, the role of the first-level manager is to absorb the abnormal conditions so the team can remain focused on the normal execution. Whether the manager resolves the symptom through a Band-Aid or solves the cause through problem solving is a situational choice, but in either scenario, they absorb the abnormal work that threatens to disrupt the flow. Consider the case of actually fighting fires. In many towns and communities, such as my own, the fire department (ours is composed of volunteers) does not have an endless stream of fires to fight. They may face a true emergency only every other day. Because of this, they can often absorb much of the abnormal work, from cleaning to fire education to parades. However, on a ladder truck in downtown Manhattan, there are near endless calls, even if many are false alarms, and because the risk is so great, those on the truck are very active. Therefore, responding to an emergency call is the normal work. The abnormal work is too important to just push out endlessly, and so other resources are dedicated to absorbing this other work.

The next level is providing surge capacity. This means that, most of the time, the nature of the team's work, as well as their capacity, allows them to execute their work, solve problems, and make improvements. However, certain periods of time reflect an increase in the overall workload, and so the improvement tends to stop. This provides the opportunity for a manager to step in and absorb some of the abnormality of the surge in work. This could be reflected in a surge of issue resolution (such as a manager taking calls in the call center to handle a large load), a surge of problems that need to be solved (as might be the case when a new system is installed to support the work), or a surge of improvement efforts when taking on a significant transformation.

This can also work in reverse where the manager steps in to perform the work while the team member steps away to solve a problem. I remember quite distinctly, a long time ago, working with Takeshi Iwata (founder of the consulting firm Shingijutsu) on a *kaizen* improvement event, and we needed a specific member from the assembly team relieved from his assignment so he could help his peers. Bob Lutz, automotive legend and at the time president of Chrysler, rolled up his sleeves and began installing sway bars into minivans. While this is an extreme example, the point was clear: the operator was more valuable to the problem-solving effort at that moment in time than the president of the company was.

It is important when stepping in as part of surge capacity to not let it become the norm. Otherwise, you simply become a member of the team and lose the broader perspective and longer time horizon you should be providing. The trick is not making the extra capacity simply an escape valve for not improving the work. If the manager steps in too easily, then instead of solving why there is a surge of problems, you may absorb the incentive to change while absorbing the work itself.

This role is most effectively played by the manager when the required surge is predictable, either based on criteria or based on a season. For example, long ago, when I worked for the energy company DTE Energy, the president would tell us all we had two jobs at the company. The first job was storm duty, and the second was whatever your business card said. His point was the abnormal condition of a big storm that knocked down wires and caused outages required everyone to stop what they were doing and pitch in, even if it just meant standing by a downed wire to make sure no one went near it while waiting for a crew.

The third level is where the manager can truly focus on problem-solving the system, be it the system of work, the culture, or the capabilities as discussed earlier. This is most effective when the work is knowledge work or when the experience of those executing the work is best suited for solving their own problems. Across the landscape of so many types of jobs, this is an increasing amount of the type of work organizations perform, whereas the type explored in the first level is decreasing due to automation and other mechanisms. At this level, the team should be set up, including their capacity, to solve many of their own problems. The manager can act as a coach but also be involved enough to observe both the work of the problems and how they are resolved. These observations allow the manager to solve problems at this more systemic level.

Problem Solving Your Problem Solving

I find it ironically comical and tragic when someone tasked with the challenge of improving a company's problem solving jumps to conclusions, throws solutions at the problem, and generally approaches the challenge in an unstructured, unscientific manner. We should be cautious of grand interventions promising to take us to the next level without even a clear articulation of what gap (or problem statement) we are attempting to close.

Instead, we should approach improving our problem solving with the same disciplined, structured, rigorous, and granular approach that we adopt in solving all our other problems. A great way to start is to think about two other precursors to problem solving: measurement and standards. As is often quoted from the Toyota Production System creator Taiichi Ohno, "Without standards, there can be no improvement." This was the focus of chapter 3. The fundamental meaning of this is that if you start introducing solutions to problems into an unstable environment full of variation, you may simply be adding more variation to the environment.

Do you want to improve the coaching of problem solving? Begin by understanding what standards you have adopted to perform this coaching, along with how well those standards have been adopted and applied. Do you want to improve your capacity to solve problems? Begin by understanding the systemic rules and conditions that set aside this capacity for problem solving today.

Measuring your problem-solving efforts is another way to help shape and drive your improvement of problem solving. The challenge is that, like almost every other process, we should be measuring not just our quantity and delivery of problem solving but also our effectiveness or quality, and our efficiency or productivity. Most problem-solving measurement focuses on the easiest thing to measure: problem solving count. This is common when there is a standard template. We also qualify problem solving as being equal to completing the template, even if it is a false effort. Quantity is best served as an indicator of activity, but when goals are set around quantity, most often the quality will naturally suffer as people rush to complete templates.

So how do you measure quality? This is quite difficult for problem solving. When problem-solving efforts are pervasive, then in aggregate, problem-solving quality should correlate quite well with your long-term overall performance. There are quite a few other factors that can disrupt this correlation, and of course, the lagging nature of any outcome performance metric makes it hard to make proactive improvements.

While neither easy nor automatic, the best mechanism to measure quality is to audit and grade actual problem-solving methods. Develop criteria for what *good* will look like for all steps of problem solving and then take a sample of your problem-solving efforts and grade them. You can't do this for all problems, as sometimes it takes as much effort to grade them as it does to actually solve the problems. However, the information it gives you helps you target the right areas of your problem-solving quality. This is why many organizations end up with different templates and tools, because they are solving their own unique quality gaps in their problem-solving efforts and the template or method is one of the potential standards on which they can implement improvements.

Finally, we can also measure our efficiency, which is best thought of as the speed of problem solving. This means discovering the average—and perhaps just as tellingly, variation or sigma—of the duration of solving a problem. Just like the quantity metric, setting a goal for yourself can lead to the wrong behaviors, such as rushing through the problem investigation just to say it is closed out faster. However, assuming you dig past the surface of the measurement with direct observation, then the speed of problem solving can tell you quite a bit. Are we allocating enough time to solve problems? Are we biting off problems that are too big? Are problem owners getting the help they need from collaborators or coaches? Are approval loops for necessary improvements too slow? The measurement won't tell you which of these systematic causes needs to be improved, but it will indicate changes in the ecosystem surrounding our problem-solving efforts that can lead to the right systematic problem solving of our problem solving.

24

Call to Action

I hope that as you have read through this book, you have captured many actionable ideas and improvements, either for yourself or your organization. If your takeaway is to update your training program and modify your problem-solving templates, then please reread the book from the beginning. I attempted to make plain that these are not where you will find leverage.

Before I jump into some recommendations, we should first acknowledge that problem solving is a lifelong pursuit. Do not try to take everything this book has to offer and jam it into your personal or organizational practice. Instead, decide where to concentrate. Narrow your focus. Just like problem solving itself, the more granular and targeted your focus, the faster you will make progress, and then you can move on to the next gap you'd like to close. You might decide to narrow your focus by just working on cultivating one capability, shaping one behavior, beginning coaching, or changing one aspect of your ecosystem. In other words, you might create change by focusing broadly on all dimensions but go fairly shallow in each section. An alternative approach is to focus on one dimension and go very deep. For example, you might decide you have a strong capability but really need to build a culture around problem solving. In that case, you might focus on section 3 about Problem-Solving Culture, as well as chapter 21 on Building Culture.

Many who read this will focus on lessons they can apply to an organization. Consultants may change some of their engagement strategies, change agents will do the same thing, and leaders will find new leverage for change. Certainly, there is great leverage in purposeful, structural, organizational change.

However, do not miss the great opportunity for self-improvement, no matter where you are on your journey. The idea of "organizational change" is a bit of a contradiction. Organizations don't change. The people inside an organization change, and when enough of them have changed to enough of a degree, then the result is organizational change. Whether you are a master, and this modifies how you teach and coach, or a beginner, and this puts you on the right path, I hope you find opportunities for personal improvement.

When I would sign copies of my first book, *The Hitchhiker's Guide to Lean,* I would often write, "Lean begins with you!" I titled this book *People Solve Problems* because it is about people, not tools and templates. People Solve Problems, and you are people. Start with improving yourself!

Acknowledgments

Without question, this part of the book is the hardest to write. There are so many people to thank, and in such profound ways, that it hardly seems like words are sufficient. There will be people I forget to thank, and I am even more certain I will not offer sufficient thanks for the many gifts I have received.

I will start with the book itself, as it took the help of many to bring it to fruition.

I would not have been able to complete this book without the organization, persistence, efforts, and encouragement of Susan Winter on my team. Her support on so many fronts has been massively appreciated. It is only appropriate that I begin with her.

There are many people who helped along the way, including Rob Worth of Exapt Press who provided the first edits and an insightful structural review. Laia Dausà illustrated the book with insight and creativity. Bethany Brown of The Cadence Group provided excellent guidance and management throughout the whole process. Gwyn Flowers of GKS Creative provided incredible cover design and layout, and Kim Bookless's detailed editing polished the final product.

Although I could include this in each section of these acknowledgments, I thank author and friend Mark Graban. His experience in blogging, podcasting, and authoring numerous books through his own lean lens has been shared freely, and he is always ready with useful advice. Our partnership on the podcast *Lean Whiskey* is an act of friendship and a truly enjoyable process.

My professional and lean learning journey brought me to write this book, and failing these acknowledgments would miss how the knowledge of this book was generated. There is no way to begin this without starting with Andy Carlino. Andy was my cofounder in my old firm and coauthor of *The Hitchhiker's Guide to Lean*. Much more than that, he was a mentor, partner, brother, and friend. Our time working side by side was not just incredibly enjoyable but also where I found my professional place in this world.

Bob Bruggeworth, CEO of Qorvo, deserves praise for being the kind of leader I always wanted to work with. In addition to writing the forward for this book, he provided me the opportunity to reignite my passion for transformation during my time inside Qorvo. Anyone who has heard me speak knows I think culture and leadership engagement are the most critical elements of success. After selling my business, I received a call from Bob, and he told me he wanted to build a Qorvo culture and he wanted to own that culture. This was music to my ears. I joined the Qorvo executive team and met tremendous people and thoroughly enjoyed my time helping a broad cadre of leaders willing to step up and lead.

I have had the great opportunity of working with over three hundred companies and countless individuals. For certain, many companies and individuals stand out as having purpose, courage, and skill to build a stronger organization. However, there are still too many to name. Most of you will know who you are. My best clients over the years have made me smarter by asking tough questions that make me think hard about difficult challenges, and I am inspired by their efforts. I thank each and every one of you, because this is why I continue my work.

On a personal level, I have many friends and family members who have supported me over the years and to this day. My in-laws, Ron and Ellen, have supported my family and me through both small and large challenges and were gracious enough to loan me their cottage where the entirety of this book was written. My parents, Jim and Wendy, provided me with the blueprint to lead a noble and high-integrity life, even if it took me a long time to learn their lessons. My children, Emma, Jack, and Ben, brought enjoyment and intention to my life, even if I was away for too much of their lives.

Finally, to my wife, Jill Triani, I owe everything. She has been my muse, and every day I wake trying to become the man she deserves to have as a husband.

About the Author

JAMIE FLINCHBAUGH is an accomplished Entrepreneur, Senior Executive, Consultant, and Board Member with 30 years of learning-oriented experience spanning a range of roles across exceptionally diverse industries and functions. Leveraging extensive operational, strategic, and consulting experience, Jamie is an invaluable asset for any company seeking to build culture, capability, leadership, and their overall operating system. As the founder of JFlinch, Jamie provides this support as a board member, advisor, coach, and speaker.

Throughout his career, Jamie has held leadership positions with JFlinch (Founder), Qorvo (Executive), Old Dutch Group LLC (Founder), Lean Learning Center (Co-Founder), Rev! Motorcycles (Co-Founder), DTE Energy (Change Agent), and Chrysler (Operational Leader). As the Founder of JFlinch, Jamie helps teams accelerate their journey by solving their challenging problems and providing the resources, education, and tools needed to make lean leaders successful. Through Old Dutch Group, Jamie invests in organizations ranging from traditional manufacturing to startups and real estate. He recently served 3 years as the Corporate Vice President (part-time) of Qorvo's Lean Journey.

During his 15 years as Co-Founder, with Andy Carlino and Dennis Pawley, of the Lean Learning Center, Jamie built the organization to become one of the premium providers of lean transformation and advisory services, with their educational programs earning the highest marks. In 2006, he co-authored the lean bestseller, *The Hitchhiker's Guide to Lean: Lessons from the Road*, and he has worked with over 300 clients spanning manufacturing, healthcare, utilities, technology, government, and professional services, including Harley-Davidson, Intel, Mars, Amazon, Crayola, Fidelity, Whirlpool, among others.

Over the last 20+ years, Jamie has helped build nearly 20 companies as a co-founder, board member, advisor, or angel investor, including co-founding the Lehigh Valley Angel Investors and acting as the initial Investment Chair. Jamie is a board member of Robinson Fans, and is a former board member of York Container Company, Orion Fleet Intelligence, S&S Cycle, PA Rush Soccer, and previously chaired the Board of Advisors for the Pawley Lean Institute at Oakland University. Jamie has been a Contributing Editor for IndustryWeek and columnist for Assembly Magazine. Jamie obtained two Master of Science in Mechanical Engineering degrees from the Massachusetts Institute of Technology and the University of Michigan, an MBA from the Massachusetts Institute of Technology, and attained his BS in Mechanical Engineering from Lehigh University, where he has served in numerous volunteer capacities. He currently resides in Bucks County, Pennsylvania with his wife and 3 children.

CPSIA information can be obtained
at www.ICGtesting.com
Printed in the USA
BVHW090022181021
619179BV00012B/535/J